NEWS 3X/ TECHNICAL REFERENCE SERIES

Bryan Meyers
series editor

Desktop Guide to

CL

Programming

by Bryan Meyers

Library of Congress Cataloging-in-Publication Data

Meyers, Bryan, 1948-
    Desktop guide to CL programming / Bryan Meyers. — 1st ed.
      p.   cm. — (NEWS 3X/400 Technical Reference Series)
    ISBN 1-882419-07-3
    1. Job Control Language (Computer program language) 2. IBM computers—
Programming I. Title. II. Series.
QA76.73.J63M49   1994
005. 4'3—dc20
                                        94-33312
                                         CIP

Copyright © 1994 by DUKE PRESS
DUKE COMMUNICATIONS INTERNATIONAL
Loveland, Colorado

This book was printed and bound in the United States of America.
First Edition, September 1994

ISBN 1-882419-07-3

ISBN 1-882419-11-1 (*NEWS 3X/400* Technical Reference Series)

To my wife, Sandy, who put up with me during yet another one of these long projects — and who kept reminding me, "You can't play today. You have to write!"

And to my mother, Lillian, who will surely keep a copy of this book on her coffee table, to show her friends — even though she nor they will understand or even care about its subject.

Acknowledgments

Several people deserve thanks for their efforts in "birthing" this book, but one stands out. Sharon Hamm spent countless hours editing and formatting my rough manuscript — and making it presentable for both the hard copy and the electronic versions. Thank you, Sharon.

Thanks also to Dave Bernard for his encouragement, Ernie Malaga for reviewing the manuscript, Paul Conte for suggesting Doc-to-Help's online Windows Help, Roger Pence for finding just the right monotype font, Steve Adams for the cover, Ann McLendon for her imaginative promotional efforts, and Jan Caufman for her back-up production assistance.

Table of Contents

Introduction

Chapter 1

Using This Book

Control Language (CL) is the primary procedural processing language for the AS/400. It is the set of commands you use to control operations and to request system-related functions. You can use CL commands either interactively, using the AS/400 command line, or you can include CL commands in a compiled program object, which you can then call.

This book is not meant to be an introduction to CL. Instead, it is oriented toward the programmer who already knows how to write CL programs. Why would you need the book if you already know how to use CL? Good question. There are well over a thousand CL commands, each of them with different parameters, and each of them with a slightly different purpose. There are also functions that you might need to perform on an ongoing basis that require specific complex CL techniques. Searching through the IBM manuals (if you have them) to find the correct command, or developing a workable technique each time you need to do a task, is not a productive use of your time.

This book contains notes, short explanations, and code segments that you can use every day in your own CL programming. What's the correct command to retrieve information from the local data area? (There are more than one.) How should you code a standard error message handler? What is the return value that identifies a diagnostic message? What rules do you need to worry about when passing a constant as a parameter? What messages can occur when you use the CVTDAT command? You'll find the answers to these and many other everyday CL questions in this book. In addition, we've included a comprehensive "short reference" that lists approximately 350 CL commands and explains the most-often-used ones, along with the files they use, and MONMSG messages.

We don't waste a lot of your time explaining why a certain technique works, or the intricacies of obscure parameter values that you probably will never use. Instead, we rely on tables, short examples, and "cut-and-paste"-able code that you can use and reuse in your own programs. We hope you'll find this "Just Do It" approach to CL programming

---

productive and useful enough that this book will find a permanent place on a corner of your desk.

CL Coding Style Standards

Chapter 2

Style Guidelines

CL, being a free-format language, does not force you into following many strict rules about how to type CL code into a source member. If you keep in mind a few style guidelines, however, you'll find your programs easier to read and maintain. Here are a few ideas:

Type variable names in lowercase.

- CL doesn't care whether you name variables with uppercase or lowercase characters. It will treat &DATE, &date, and &Date as the same variable. But to make your source code more readable, type variable names in lowercase.

Use positional keyword notation for common commands.

- Many CL commands are more readable if you omit keyword notation for certain parameters and use positional notation instead. For example, the MONMSG command is more readable if you omit the MSGID and CMPDTA keywords:

```
MONMSG   CPF9801 EXEC(RETURN)
```

Unfortunately, the seldom-used CMPDTA parameter is the second positional parameter in the MONMSG command, while the often-used EXEC parameter is third. You cannot, therefore, use positional notation for the EXEC parameter unless you include the CMPDTA parameter. The following command will not work:

```
MONMSG   CPF9801 RETURN
```

You can, however, include the *N null value for the CMPDTA parameter if you want to specify the EXEC parameter in positional notation:

```
MONMSG   CPF9801 *N RETURN
```

Usually, though, you'll find that the EXEC parameter is specified in keyword notation.

Other common commands that are easy to read in positional notation are

---

```
DCL      &pgmvar  *DEC  (5 0)
CHGVAR   &pgmvar  12345
IF       (&answer *EQ 'Y') DO
GOTO     YES
ELSE     DO
```

If a command parameter allows expressions, you must enclose the expressions in parentheses:

```
CHGVAR   &pgmvar1  (&pgmvar + 12345)
```

Begin labels in column 1.

- Labels should clearly identify entry points into specific areas of the CL program. To find labels easily, always begin them in column 1 of the program source. Lend readability to a program by placing a label alone on a line, with no other code.

Indent your code.

- To help identify the code in a DO group, you should always indent the code:

```
IF      (&option *EQ 1) DO
        CALL   PGMA
        CALL   PGMB
        ENDDO
ELSE DO
        CALL   PGMC
        CALL   PGMD
        ENDDO
```

Line up your code.

- Along with indentation, you can help your program's readability by lining up successive lines of code and allowing blank lines in the code to break it into logical groups.

  Try to code an entire command on one line; if a specification must span more than one line of code, follow these two guidelines:

  — Be sure the + continuation characters in the program line up vertically in the program.

  — Limit the number of command parameters to one per line.

The following example illustrates how these guidelines lend to the readability of the code:

```
RMVMSG      MSGKEY(&$msgkey)

SNDPGMMSG   MSGID(&$msgid)                  +
            MSGF(&$msgflib/&$msgf)          +
            MSGDTA(&$msgdta)                +
            MSGTYPE(*DIAG)
GOTO        ERROR2
```

Use DO Groups with MONMSG, IF, ELSE.

- It's good programming practice to always use DO groups in connection with command-level MONMSG commands, even if you will only execute a single command because of the error. The IF and ELSE commands should also always specify DO groups. This technique lends to the program's ease of maintenance by allowing you the freedom to easily insert commands into a DO group. It also makes the specification easier to read, by generally limiting it to one line. Program-level (global) MONMSG commands, however, do not allow a DO group.

Use shorthand with care.

- The concatenation operations support a shorthand notation. Instead of *CAT, *TCAT, and *BCAT, you can use ||, |<, and |>, respectively. Consequently, both of the following commands accomplish the same end:

```
CHGVAR   &message                            +
         ('Today is' *BCAT &today *TCAT '.')

CHGVAR   &message ('Today is' |> &today |< '.')
```

While the special symbols make the code more compact, they also make it harder to read and understand. Avoid the short versions.

CL also allows short versions of the *EQ, *NE, *OR, *GT, *LT, and *NOT operators. For example, the following expressions are equivalent:

```
(&pgmvar *NE 0)
(&pgmvar ¬= 0)
```

Again, the symbols hide the true purpose of the code. In the case of the "not" symbol (¬), the symbol may not translate to the same symbol on all platforms, such as PC-DOS, so it is especially insidious.

The substring and binary functions also have abbreviated versions, but in these cases the shorter versions don't hide the purpose of the code. You can specify either %SUBSTRING or %SST to indicate a portion of a character string. For the binary function, code either %BINARY or %BIN.

```
CHGVAR   &library %SUBSTRING(&fullname 11 10)
CHGVAR   &library %SST(&fullname 11 10)
```

Reuse code.

- One of the keys to coding efficiencies is to reuse existing, tested code whenever possible. In code segments or modules that you plan to reuse, you can facilitate reuse by using a variable naming convention that is unlikely to duplicate variable names among various code segments. In this book, program variables that are likely to be reused are preceded by &$ instead of a lone ampersand (&):

```
DCL   &$pgmvar   *DEC  (5 0)
DCL   &$msgid    *CHAR 7
```

Another good code reuse technique is to define variables to represent frequently used literals, or literals with obscure meanings:

```
      /* RTNTYPE for *COMP (Completion) message */
DCL   &$msg_comp *CHAR 2 VALUE('01')
```

Declaring Variables

Chapter 3

Before a CL program can use a program variable, it must define the variable. The DCL (Declare) and DCLF (Declare File) commands define variables. DCL explicitly defines a variable. The DCLF command implicitly defines all the fields in a file as program variables. Variable names begin with an ampersand (&) followed by up to 10 characters. The first character must be alphabetic (A-Z); remaining characters are alphanumeric.

CL supports three data types: *CHAR, *DEC, and *LGL.

Type:		*CHAR	*DEC	*LGL
Description:		Character string	Packed decimal number	Logical flag
Valid values:		Any characters	Numbers only	'0' (false, off), or '1' (true, on)
Length:		1-9999 bytes	1-15 digits, including 0-9 decimal places	Always 1 byte
Default initial value		Blanks	0	'0'
Default length	No initial value specified	LEN(32)	LEN(15 5)	Always 1 byte
	Initial value is specified	Length of initial value, up to LEN(3000)	Length of initial value	Always 1 byte

Declaring Variables in a Command Processing Program

If a CL program is to be used as a command processing program (CPP), you must take care to declare the CL variables to correspond to the data type and length that the command definition object (CDO) specifies for the parameter. Since commands support more data types than does CL, unsupported data types map to one of the three CL data types. These are the parameter types used most often:

Command Definition		CL Declaration
PARM TYPE(*CHAR)	LEN(n)	DCL *CHAR n[1]
PARM TYPE(*CMDSTR)	LEN(n)	DCL *CHAR n[1]
PARM TYPE(*CNAME)	LEN(n)	DCL *CHAR n[1]
PARM TYPE(*DATE)		DCL *CHAR 7
PARM TYPE(*DEC)	LEN(x y)	DCL *DEC (x y)
PARM TYPE(*GENERIC)	LEN(n)	DCL *CHAR n[1]
PARM TYPE(*HEX)	LEN(n)	DCL *CHAR n[1]
PARM TYPE(*INT2)		DCL *CHAR 2[2]
PARM TYPE(*INT4)		DCL *CHAR 4[2]
PARM TYPE(*LGL)		DCL *LGL
PARM TYPE(*NAME)	LEN(n)	DCL *CHAR n[1]
PARM TYPE(*SNAME)	LEN(n)	DCL *CHAR n[1]
PARM TYPE(*TIME)		DCL *CHAR 6

[1] For these data types, if the CL variable is shorter than the command parameter, the command parameter is truncated.

[2] Use the built-in %BIN function in the CL program to convert these data types to decimal values.

Using the CHGVAR Command

Chapter 4

The CHGVAR (Change Variable) Command

The CHGVAR (Change Variable) command changes the value of a CL program variable. The command takes the following form:

```
CHGVAR &program-variable   value
```

You can change the value of the variable to a constant, to the value of another variable, or to the value of an expression. You can also use the %SST and %BIN built-in functions with the CHGVAR command, and you can retrieve the contents of the local data area using CHGVAR.

The following rules apply to the CHGVAR command:

- The value of a logical variable must be '1' or '0'. The value of a decimal variable must be a decimal number. Character variables can accept either character or decimal values.

- When you specify a decimal value for a character variable, the value is right-aligned and padded with leading zeroes. If the number is negative, a minus sign (-) is placed in the leftmost position of the character variable.

- When you specify a character value for a decimal variable, the value is aligned with the decimal point in the proper position for the decimal variable. If the character value contains a leading sign (+ or -), it is incorporated into the decimal value. The character value must not contain intervening blanks. The character value can contain more characters to the right of the decimal point than the decimal variable allows; excess characters will be truncated. The decimal variable must be large enough, however, to hold all the characters to the left of the decimal, or an error will occur.

You can use CL's %SST and %BIN built-in functions with either the VAR or VALUE parameter of the CHGVAR command. To change the value of a portion of a *CHAR variable, specify the %SST function in the VAR (i.e., the first) parameter:

```
CHGVAR %SST(&program-variable position length)  +
       value
```

To change the value of a variable to match a substring of another
*CHAR variable, specify the %SST function in the VALUE (i.e., the
second) parameter:

```
CHGVAR &variable-1                              +
       %SST(&variable-2 position length)
```

To convert a binary number in a *CHAR variable to a decimal variable,
specify the %BIN function in the VALUE parameter:

```
CHGVAR &dec-var            +
       %BIN(&char-var 1 2)
```

To convert the other direction, specify the %BIN in the VAR parameter:

```
CHGVAR %BIN(&char-var 1 2)  +
       &dec-var
```

Using Expressions

Chapter 5

Types of CL Expressions

Many parameters, elements, or qualifiers in CL commands can be represented by expressions. In particular, the CHGVAR and IF commands frequently use expressions:

```
CHGVAR  &salary  (&salary * 1.1)
IF       (&answer *EQ 'Y') DO
```

CL supports four types of expressions: (1) arithmetic, (2) character, (3) relational, and (4) logical.

Expressions usually consist of two or more operands separated by an operator, which indicates the action or evaluation to take place on the operands:

Arithmetic expression	(&salary * 1.1)
Character expression	(&firstname *BCAT &lastname)
Relational expression	(&salary > 50000)
Logical expression	(&in50 *AND &in51)

Arithmetic expressions consist of decimal constants and/or decimal variables on either side of an arithmetic operator. The result of an arithmetic expression is a decimal value. The following common mathematic symbols are also CL's arithmetic operators:

+ addition
- substraction
* multiplication
/ division

Character string expressions consist of character strings, character variables, or the %SST built-in function, on either side of a concatenation operator (*CAT, *BCAT, or *TCAT). For more information about character string expressions, see *Character String Expressions and Concatenation*, page 13.

Relational expressions evaluate the relationship between arithmetic, character, or logical operands. The result of a relational expression is either a true condition ('1') or a false condition ('0'). The relational

---

operator predefined values, along with their symbolic representations, are

*EQ	=	Equal
*GT	>	Greater than
*LT	<	Less than
*GE	>=	Greater than or equal
*LE	<=	Less than or equal
*NE	¬=	Not equal
*NG	¬>	Not greater than
*NL	¬<	Not less than

Logical expressions specify the logical relationship between operands. A logical expression can consist of only one operand, or of two operands separated by a logical operator. The result of a logical expression is either a true condition ('1') or a false condition ('0'). The logical operator predefined values, along with their symbolic representations, are

*AND	&	And (Both operands are true)
*OR	|	Or (Either operand is true)
*NOT	¬	Not (Negates *AND, *OR)

A complex expression contains more than two operands and more than a single operator. For example, the following is a complex expression:

```
(&salary * 1.1 + &bonus)
```

CL will use the following order of evaluation when evaluating a complex expression:

1. +, - (when used as signs with decimal values), ***NOT, ¬**
2. ***, /**
3. +, - (when used as operators in expressions)
4. ***CAT, ||, *BCAT, |>, *TCAT, |<**
5. ***EQ, =, *GT, >, *LT, <, GE, >=, *LE, <=, *NE, ¬=, *NG, ¬>, *NL, ¬<**
6. ***AND**
7. ***OR**

When an expression contains operators of the same order, CL performs the operations from left to right. But you can alter the order of evaluation using parentheses to group those portions of an expression that you want to evaluate together.

There is a limit to the complexity of expressions that you can use within CL. Not all command parameters will allow an expression. Sometimes a parameter that accepts *CHAR data will not accept an expression; and only rarely will a *DEC parameter accept a numeric expression.

Character String Expressions and Concatenation

Chapter 6

Concatenation Operations

In addition to arithmetic expressions, you can use the CL *concatenate operator* (*CAT) to specify character string expressions for the VALUE parameter of the CHGVAR command. *CAT joins two character strings and/or values together, allowing you to connect multiple values and assign them as a variable's value. Each value specified in a character string expression must be either a character constant or a character variable.

Two variations of the *CAT operation make it even more useful. *TCAT (Concatenate with truncation) removes all trailing blanks from the first value, then connects the two values. *BCAT (Concatenate with a blank) also removes trailing blanks from the first value, then joins the two values; but *BCAT always inserts a single blank between the values. Neither *TCAT not *BCAT remove leading blanks from the second value. The following figure provides examples of character string expressions (• represents a blank).

Length and beginning values of *CHAR type variables:

```
LEN(23)    &a  =   •••••••••••••••••••••••
LEN(10)    &b  =   John••••••
LEN(1)     &c  =   I
LEN(10)    &d  =   Smith•••••
```

CHGVAR command	Resulting value of &a
CHGVAR &a + (&b *CAT &c *CAT &d)	John••••••ISmith•••••
CHGVAR &a + (&b *TCAT &c *TCAT &d)	JohnISmith••••••••••••
CHGVAR &a + (&b *BCAT &c *BCAT &d)	John•I•Smith••••••••••
CHGVAR &a + ('Dear' *BCAT &b *BCAT &d + *TCAT ':')	Dear•John•Smith:•••••

You can also represent the concatentation operators using symbols, if you wish:

*CAT	‖
*BCAT	|>
*TCAT	|<

Most programmers, however, find the spelled-out operators easier to read and understand than the symbols.

Using the %SUBSTRING Function

Chapter 7

The %SST Function

In a CL program you can use the built-in %SUBSTRING (%SST) function to place a portion of an existing character CL variable into another variable, or to evaluate or process a portion of a character variable. The substring begins at a starting position you specify and carries on for a length you specify. The %SST function uses the following syntax:

```
%SST(&CL-variable start length)
```

The start position and length can be either literals or CL variables.

You can use the substring function with either parameter of the CHGVAR (Change Variable) command:

```
CHGVAR &library %SST(&qualname 11 10)
CHGVAR %SST(&qualname 11 10) &library
```

You can also use the %SST function in an expression with the IF command:

```
IF (%SST(&qualname 11 10) *EQ 'QGPL') DO
.
.
.
ENDDO
```

CL will pad the operands in the expression to a common length to make any comparisons; in the above example, positions 11-20 of &qualname will be compared with 'QGPL   '.

Use %SST to remove leading zeros.

In the following example of the %SST function, CL will replace with blanks any leading zeros in the CL variable &$nbr_var, a character variable that contains a right-adjusted number:

```
                          DCL  &$nbr_var *CHAR
                          DCL  &$counter *DEC  (3 0) VALUE(1)
                            .
                            .
                            .
              LOOP:
                          IF (&$counter *GT 7) GOTO LOOP /* Length of &$nbr_var = 7 *
                          IF (%SST(&$nbr_var &$counter 1) *GT 0) GOTO ENDLOOP
                          IF (%SST(&$nbr_var &$counter 1) *EQ 0) DO
                             CHGVAR (%SUBSTRING(&$nbr_var &$counter 1)) ' '
                             CHGVAR  &$counter  (&$counter + 1)
                             GOTO   LOOP
                             ENDDO
              ENDLOOP:
```

Binary Values and Hexadecimal Notation

Chapter 8

Hexadecimal Numbers

Occasions may occur when it is necessary to initialize a *CHAR variable to a value that cannot be represented by a character from your computer keyboard. In these cases, you can set the value of the variable to a hexadecimal number.

The set of hexadecimal numbers contains the values 0-9 and A-F. Hexadecimal numbers, although not often used in CL, can be used for such things as manipulating screen attributes, processing lists of values, and assisting in data comparison operations. To specify hex notation, CL uses an X, followed by a quoted character string consisting of pairs of hexadecimal numbers. For example, if you want to initialize a *CHAR variable to the hexadecimal value of FFFF, you would enter the following DCL statement:

```
DCL  &$hex_ff *CHAR 2 VALUE(X'FFFF')
```

For information about passing hexadecimal information between programs, see *Using Hexadecimal Notation To Pass Decimal Parameters,* page 25.

The %BINARY Function

Hexadecimal notation is also commonly used with CL's built-in %BINARY (%BIN) function. You can use the %BIN function to interpret the contents of a *CHAR variable in a CL program as a binary number. The *CHAR variable must be either 2 or 4 characters long. Typically, you will use the %BIN function with either an IF expression or the CHGVAR command. Like the %SST function, %BIN begins at a starting position you specify and carries on for a length you specify. The %BIN function uses the following syntax:

```
%BIN(&CL-variable start length)
```

For example, in the following code, the value of the &$decimal variable will be 193 (X'C1').When the code ends, the &$hex variable will be 195 (X'C3'):

```
DCL   &$decimal *DEC (5 0)
DCL   &$hex      *CHAR 2     VALUE(X'00C1')
.
.
.
CHGVAR &$decimal %BIN(&$hex)
.
.
.
IF    (&$decimal = 193) DO
       CHGVAR %BIN(&$hex) VALUE(&$decimal + 2)
ENDDO
```

You can also use the %BIN function in an expression with the IF command:

```
DCL   &$hex_c1  *CHAR 2     VALUE(X'00C1')
.
.
.
IF    (%BIN(&$hex_c1) = 193) DO
.
.
.
ENDDO
```

(To see some equivalent decimal, hexadecimal, and binary representations, see *Hexadecimal Collating Sequence*, page 99.)

To use many APIs in CL, you must convert binary numbers to decimal numbers.

The IBM-supplied application program interfaces (APIs) make extensive use of binary numbers to receive parameters and to pass values back to their calling programs. To use these APIs with CL, you must first convert the binary numbers to decimal numbers, using the CHGVAR command, as shown above.

To process list parameters in a command processing program, you must use the %BIN function. For more information, see *Processing Lists*, page 87.

A 2-byte character variable can hold signed binary integer values from -32768 through 32767. A 4-byte character variable can hold signed binary integer values from -2147483648 through 2147483647.

Using Data Areas

Chapter 9

The RTVDTAARA and CHGDTAARA Commands

A CL program can retrieve, use, and change the information in data areas with the RTVDTAARA (Retrieve Data Area) and CHGDTAARA (Change Data Area) commands. You can use the RTVDTAARA command to copy the contents of all or part of a data area into a CL program variable. The CHGDTAARA command can change the contents of a data area.

To move the contents of a data area into a CL variable, use the RTVDTAARA command. For example, to move the first 10 bytes of a data area named QGPL/SBMDTA into a CL variable called &library, use the following command:

```
RTVDTAARA   (QGPL/SBMDTA (1 10))   +
            RTNVAR(&library)
```

To change the contents of a data area, use the CHGDTAARA command. To change the value of the first 10 bytes of the QGPL/SBMDTA data area to match the value of the &library variable, use the following command:

```
CHGDTAARA   (QGPL/SBMDTA (1 10))   +
            VALUE(&library)
```

The local data area and the group job data area are special data areas.

CL also supports several special data areas, including the local data area and the group job data area. Every job has a local data area (1024 bytes) associated with it; this data area is assigned to the job and is not accessible from other jobs. If the job is a group job, there is also a group job data area (512 bytes) associated with all the jobs in the group. CL refers to the local data area using the special value *LDA, and to the group job data area using the special value *GDA. For example, to move the first 10 bytes of the local data area into a CL variable named &library, you would specify the following command:

```
RTVDTAARA   (*LDA (1 10))    +
            RTNVAR(&library)
```

You can use the CHGVAR command with the local data area.

In the case of the local data area, you can also use the CHGVAR command to change or read the contents of the data area. The following CL commands are equivalent:

```
CHGDTAARA   (*LDA (1 10))    +
            VALUE(&library)

CHGVAR      %SST(*LDA 1 10)  +
            &library
```

as are these commands:

```
RTVDTAARA   (*LDA (1 10))    +
            RTNVAR(&library)

CHGVAR      &library         +
            %SST(*LDA 1 10)
```

The CALL Command

Chapter 10

Passing Parameters with the CALL Command

The CALL command invokes the execution of a program, passing information to the called program as parameter values. The CALL command takes the following syntax:

```
CALL library/program PARM(parameter-list)
```

The PGM statement in the called program accepts the parameter values by specifying the CL variables to contain them:

```
PGM (parameter-list)
```

The following rules apply to the CALL command and the passed parameters:

- You can pass up to 40 parameters.

- The parameters can be constants (character, numeric, or logical) or CL program variables.

- Parameter values are passed in the order in which they appear on the CALL command. The PGM statement (in the called program) must specify the receiving variables in the same order.

- The CL variables in the called program need not have the same name as the CL variables passed by the calling program.

- You must declare the receiving variables in the called program.

- If you pass variables to a called program, the receiving variables (in the called program) must be declared with the same data type and length as in the calling program.

- Variables are passed by address. If you change the value of a variable in the called program, the change will be reflected in the calling program's variable at the same memory location.

- Constants are passed by value. If you pass a constant to a called program, then change the variable that accepts the constant value, there will be no effect in the calling program. For more information on passing constant values, see *Passing Constant Parameters Between Programs,* page 23.

- When CL calls C/400 programs, it always passes parameters by value, as a null terminated string, whether they are variables or constants.

- Some commands, such as SBMJOB (Submit Job), contain a command string parameter (TYPE(*CMDSTR)) that allows you to pass a command as a parameter value. If you use the SBMJOB command in a CL program to submit a job to batch, and if the CMD parameter includes program variables, the system will convert the variables to constants before it executes the SBMJOB command. For these variables, you must be sure to follow the rules for passing constants.

Passing Constant Parameters Between Programs

Chapter 11

Rules for Passing Constants

You can pass constants from one CL program to another program, subject to the following rules:

- Character constants up to 32 bytes long are passed to the called program with a length of 32, padded on the right with blanks if necessary.

  ```
  CALL program PARM('character string')
  ```

- Character constants more than 32 bytes long are passed to the called program with their exact length. You must be careful to declare the receiving variable in the called program with the same length as the constant in the calling program. If the receiving parameter is longer than the constant, the value of the parameter may include undesired data from the next parameter in the called program.

- When passing character constants, never declare the parameter variable longer than 32 characters, unless you are certain that you will always pass the correct number of characters.

- Decimal constants are passed to the calling program with a length of LEN(15 5) (i.e., 15 digits including 5 decimal places).

  ```
  CALL program PARM(3.14159)
  ```

  In this example, the parameter in the receiving program *must* be declared as LEN(15 5).

- To pass a decimal constant with a declared length other than LEN(15 5), pass it in hexadecimal notation:

  ```
  CALL program PARM(X'31416F')
  CALL program PARM(X'0012995F')
  CALL program PARM(X'12995D')
  ```

In the first example, the decimal constant *3.1416* is passed to a program that will accept the parameter into a decimal variable defined as *DEC (5 4). If the receiving variable is defined as *DEC (5 0), it would be received as *31416*, without a decimal point. In the second example, the decimal constant *129.95* is passed to a program that will accept the parameter as *DEC (7 2). The third example shows how to pass a negative number. In this case, the decimal constant *129.95-* is passed to a program that will accept the parameter as *DEC (5 2).

- To pass a numeric value as a character constant, pass it as a quoted string.

- Logical constants (i.e., '1' or '0') are passed just as character constants are.

Using Hexadecimal Notation To Pass Decimal Parameters

Chapter 12

Specifying the Value of a Decimal Constant

There will be times, when you are testing or debugging a program that receives parameters, that you will want to call the program from a command line, even though under normal circumstances the program would be called from another program. When you CALL a program from the command line, however, you can pass only constants for parameter values. If the program you want to CALL requires that you pass it a decimal-type parameter, you must have defined that decimal variable within the CL program as *DEC (15 5). Herein lies a problem: Many times, this declaration may not fit your particular application.

For these cases, you can use hexadecimal notation to specify the value of a decimal constant when using the CALL command. Remember that CL passes decimals in packed format. By using hex notation to specify decimals, you can emulate the packed format. Consider the following example:

```
CALL  MYPROGRAM PARM(X'000000000500000F')
```

In this example, the decimal constant 5 is passed to a program that will accept the parameter into a variable defined as *DEC (15 5). This would be the same as specifying the following command:

```
CALL  MYPROGRAM PARM(5)
```

You can also use this notation to pass decimal parameters that are *not* defined as *DEC (15 5). Consider the following examples:

```
CALL  MYPROGRAM PARM(X'31416F')
CALL  MYPROGRAM PARM(X'12995D')
```

In the first example, the decimal constant *3.1416* is passed to a program that will accept the parameter into a decimal variable defined as *DEC (5 4). If the receiving variable is defined as *DEC (5 0), it would be received as *31416*, without a decimal point. The second example shows how to pass a negative number. In this case, the decimal constant *129.95-* is passed to a program that will accept the parameter as *DEC (5 2).

There are a few rules to keep in mind when using hexadecimal notation to emulate packed decimals:

- The constant must be preceded by an *X* and must be enclosed in a quoted string.

- The quoted string can contain only the numbers 0-9 and a trailing sign (F or D).

- The quoted string must contain an even number of hexadecimal numbers. Each pair of numbers will be packed into a single byte.

- The quoted string must end in an *F* for a positive number, or a *D* for a negative number.

Normally you would use hex notation to emulate packed decimals only when testing or debugging. For this purpose, hex notation will give you the added flexibility of not having to declare your decimal variables as *DEC (15 5). Within a program, however, the need for hex notation is eliminated by the capability to pass decimal variables other than those defined as *DEC (15 5).

Using the TFRCTL Command

Chapter 13

The TFRCTL (Transfer Control) Command

The TFRCTL (Transfer Control) comand can be used to call a program, and pass parameters to the called program. In this respect, TFRCTL works just like the CALL command. Unlike the CALL command, however, TFRCTL calls a program, then removes the transferring (calling) program from the program call stack. Using TFRCTL may improve performance by reducing the size of the process access group of a job. TFRCTL is valid only within a CL program. The TFRCTL command has the following format:

```
TFRCTL PGM(library/program) PARM(parameter-list)
```

In addition to the normal rules for passing parameters between programs, the parameters passed by the TFRCTL command are subject to the following restrictions:

- They must be CL variables.
- They must have already been passed to the transferring CL program as parameters.

When the called program ends or returns, control returns to the previous program in the call stack, *not* to the transferring program (since it is no longer in the call stack).

Command Prompting

Chapter 14

Using Command Prompting in a CL Program

Within a CL program that is designed to run interactively, you can include simple command prompting to enhance the flexibility of the program. Using the question mark (?) character, you can control the display of a prompt screen, as well as control what fields of the prompt the user can modify. In effect, you are allowing the user of the program to change the CL command as the program runs. The user will see the same prompted command parameters that (s)he would see when keying a command then pressing the F4=Prompt key.

The question mark (?) invokes prompting.

To invoke prompting, simply precede the command with a question mark. The following code, for example, would prompt for the SAVLIB (Save Library) CL command:

```
?SAVLIB  LIB(QGPL)
```

When this command is included in an interactive CL program, the user will be presented with the command prompt for the SAVLIB command. Because the LIB parameter has an assigned value (in this case, QGPL), the user cannot modify the library to be saved. Specifying a value for a command parameter within the program prohibits the user from changing that parameter. The field is displayed on the prompt, but is not input-capable. The user can, however, modify all the other fields of the SAVLIB command prompt.

You cannot include the command prompting character (?) in a program that will run as a batch job. Prompting cannot be used on commands contained in an IF, ELSE, or MONMSG command. You can, however, use prompting on commands contained within DO groups associated with an IF, ELSE, or MONMSG command. You cannot prompt for the following CL commands within a CL program:

```
CALL
CHGVAR
DCL
DCLF
DO
ELSE
ENDDO
ENDPGM
ENDRCV
IF
GOTO
MONMSG
PGM
RVCF
RETURN
SNDF
SNDRCVF
TFRCTL
WAIT
```

Message CPF6801 signals the user pressed F3 or F12.

If a CL program presents a command prompt to the user, it is *always* the user's prerogative to press F3=Exit or F12=Cancel to exit from the prompt. If this occurs, the command is not executed; and an escape message, CPF6801, is sent to the program. You should *always* monitor for this escape message whenever you use command prompting in a CL program, as the following example demonstrates:

```
?SAVLIB  LIB(QGPL)
MONMSG    CPF6801 EXEC(RETURN)
```

Here's an effective use of the CMPDTA parameter.

The above example is one of the few that could, if you wish, make effective use of the CMPDTA parameter of the MONMSG command. You can monitor for CMPDTA('F12') to determine whether the user pressed F3 or F12 to exit the command, then take appropriate action, if you need to differentiate between the two keys.

Not only may you provide prompting for CL commands within a CL program, but you may selectively determine which command parameters will be shown to the user on the prompt display and to what extent the user will be able to modify the parameters. This *selective prompting* can be used in any CL program that will run interactively. To implement selective prompting, precede specific command parameter keywords with special selective prompting character sequences. The following table describes the prompting character sequences most frequently used (There are others, but they are reserved for IBM's use):

Prompt	Value Displayed	Input Allowed
??KEYWORD()	Default	Yes
??KEYWORD(VALUE)	Value	Yes
?*KEYWORD()	Default	No
?*KEYWORD(VALUE)	Value	No
?-KEYWORD()	Parameter not displayed; command will use default	No
?-KEYWORD(VALUE)	Parameter not displayed; command will use value	No

In the following example, the user is prompted for the LIB and DEV parameters of the SAVLIB command. Either parameter can be changed; no other parameters will be shown.

```
SAVLIB    ??LIB(QGPL) ??DEV(TAP01)
MONMSG    CPF6801 EXEC(RETURN)
```

Notice that the prompting character (?) does not precede the command itself. When selective prompting characters are used within a command, the command itself need not be preceded by a question mark. However, if the command is not preceded by a question mark, the only fields displayed on the command prompt will be those that are specified on the command. This can be an effective way to reduce the number of parameters that are shown on some commands with many parameters.

In the following example, the user is prompted for the DEV parameter of the SAVLIB command. The value for the LIB parameter is shown, but cannot be changed by the user:

```
SAVLIB    ?*LIB(QGPL) ??DEV()
MONMSG    CPF6801 EXEC(RETURN)
```

Specifying ??DEV() indicates that you do not want to assign any initial value to this parameter, but want to let it default to the parameter default value, in this case a blank. But because DEV is a required parameter for the SAVLIB command, the user is forced to supply a value for it.

When you use the ?- characters to hide parameters during prompting, you must precede the command itself with a question mark (?). Usually, when you use ?- characters, you will want to specify *all* the possible command parameters, so you have more control over which ones can be changed and which ones cannot.

When working with selective prompting, you must adhere to and understand a few rules:

- A prompted command parameter must use keyword notation instead of positional notation.

- Blanks cannot appear between the selective prompting characters (??, ?*, ?-) and the parameter keyword.

- Any parameter value specified by the prompt, or supplied by the user, will be used in the execution of the command. If a value is not specified on the prompt and not specified by the user, the parameter default value will be used.

- If a CL program variable is used as a command parameter value that is changeable by the user, a change to the prompt does *not* change the value of the program variable. But the command will be executed with the changed value supplied by the user, and not with the value stored in the variable. If the user does not change the command parameter value, the value of the program variable will be used in the execution of the command.

Allocating Objects

Chapter 15

Using the ALCOBJ (Allocate Object) Command

The AS/400 allocates objects on demand. Whenever a job needs an object, it automatically allocates it, uses it, then de-allocates the object. You can, however, use the ALCOBJ (Allocate object) command to pre-allocate an object before a job needs it. To allocate an object, you must have object existence authority, object management authority, or operational authority for the object.

You can allocate an object with one or more of five lock states:

*EXCL	The system allocates the object exclusively to the allocating job. No other jobs can use the object.
*EXCLRD	The system allocates the object to the allocating job, but other jobs can read the object. This state prevents other jobs from updating or changing the object.
*SHRUPD	The allocating job shares the object with other jobs which may read, update or change the object.
*SHRNUP	The allocating job shares the object with other jobs, but they cannot update or change the object.
*SHRRD	The allocating job shares the object with other jobs, which can allocate the object for any state other than *EXCL.

The following table shows combinations of lock states that are valid among jobs using an object.

	*EXCL	*EXCLRD	*SHRNUP	*SHRUPD	*SHRRD
*EXCL	No	No	No	No	No
*EXCLRD	No	No	No	No	Yes
*SHRNUP	No	No	Yes	No	Yes
*SHRUPD	No	No	No	Yes	Yes
*SHRRD	No	Yes	Yes	Yes	Yes

The following table shows common AS/400 object types, and the valid lock states for each type.

OBJTYPE	*EXCL	*EXCLRD	*SHRNUP	*SHRUPD	*SHRRD
*DTAARA	Yes	Yes	Yes	Yes	Yes
*DTAQ	Yes	Yes	Yes	Yes	Yes
*DEVD	No	Yes	No	No	No
*FILE	Yes	Yes	Yes	Yes	Yes
*LIB	No	Yes	Yes	Yes	Yes
*MENU	Yes	Yes	Yes	Yes	Yes
*MSGQ	Yes	No	No	No	Yes
*MOD	Yes	Yes	Yes	Yes	Yes
*PNLGRP	Yes	Yes	No	No	No
*PGM	Yes	Yes	No	No	Yes
*SBSD	Yes	No	No	No	No
*USRSPC	Yes	Yes	Yes	Yes	Yes

Using the DLCOBJ Command

The system automatically deallocates objects at the end of a routing step, but you may use the DLCOBJ (Deallocate object) command to explicitly deallocate an object as soon as your job can release it. If you have used more than one ALCOBJ command for an object, you cannot completely deallocate the object with one DLCOBJ command. Each ALCOBJ requires a corresponding DLCOBJ command.

You can use multiple pairs of ALCOBJ/DLCOBJ commands.

To change the lock state of an object during a job, you can use more than one pair of ALCOBJ/DLCOBJ commands. For example, the following code would change the lock state of a file from *EXCL to *EXCLRD:

```
ALCOBJ   OBJ((file_name *FILE *EXCL))
    .
    .
    .
ALCOBJ   OBJ((file_name *FILE *EXCLRD))
DLCOBJ   OBJ((file_name *FILE *EXCL))
    .
    .
    .
DLCOBJ   OBJ((file_name *FILE *EXCLRD))
```

Notice that the code allocates the object with its new lock state before deallocating the old lock state. This sequence ensures that the job will not "lose" the object to another job.

Using File Overrides

Chapter 16

Common File Override Commands

Sometimes you need to make minor changes in the way a program functions without recompiling the program. Maybe it's necessary to change the name of a file, the name of the file member that is processed, or some other attribute of a database or printer file. To accomplish these minor changes, use file overrides; the most often used file override commands are

- OVRDBF (Override with Database File)
- OVRPRTF (Override with Printer File)

Other less-used override commands are

- OVRDKTF (Override with Diskette File)
- OVRDSPF (Override with Display File)
- OVRICFDEVE (Override with Intersystem Communications Function Program Device Entry)
- OVRICFF (Override with Intersystem Communications Function File)
- OVRMSGF (Override with Message File)
- OVRSAVF (Override with Save File)
- OVRTAPF (Override with Tape File)

See the *CL Command Summary* starting on page 107 for an explanation of some of these commands.

Use CHGxxx to permanently change an object.

To permanently change the attributes of an object, use the appropriate CHGxxx command instead of an override. Nearly any attributes you can specify when you create or change an object you can also specify with an override command when you want to temporarily change the processing of an object. An override does not affect the attributes of the object itself. It affects only the way the overriding job processes the object.

Use OVRDBF with database files.

Use the OVRDBF (Override Database File) command to redirect your program to use a database file other than one it was compiled with, or to temporarily change the processing attributes of a file. These are common uses for the OVRDBF command:

- To specify the member to be processed in a multimember file:

```
OVRDBF FILE(overridden-file)  +
       MBR(member)
```

- To specify the file to be processed among several identically named files in the library list, or to open a file by a different name:

```
OVRDBF FILE(overridden-file)  +
       TOFILE(library/file)
```

- To process all the members in a file:

```
OVRDBF FILE(overridden-file)  +
       MBR(*ALL)
```

- To enable a CL program to read a database file randomly by record number or by key:

```
OVRDBF FILE(overridden-file)   +
       POSITION(file-position)
```

- To specify a shared open data path for a file:

```
OVRDBF FILE(overridden-file)  +
       SHARE(*YES)
```

Use OVRPRTF with printer files.

Use the OVRPRTF command to to temporarily change the processing attributes of a printer file. These are common uses for the OVRPRTF command:

- To redirect printed output to a printer or output queue other than the one where a report usually prints:

```
OVRPRTF FILE(overridden-file)     +
        DEV(device)               +
        OUTQ(library/output-queue)
```

- To temporarily change the page size of a report:

```
OVRPRTF FILE(overridden-file)          +
        PAGESIZE(page-length           +
                 page-width            +
                 unit-of-measure)      +
        OVRFLW(overflow-line-number)
```

- To temporarily change the line and character spacing:

```
OVRPRTF FILE(overridden-file)    +
        LPI(lines-per-inch)      +
        CPI(characters-per-inch)
```

- To specify text to be printed at the bottom of each page of a report:

```
OVRPRTF FILE(overridden-file)  +
        PRTTXT(printed-text)
```

- To specify the number of copies of a report to print:

```
OVRPRTF FILE(overridden-file)   +
        COPIES(number-of-copies)
```

- To hold a report on an output queue, or save it on the output queue after printing:

```
OVRPRTF FILE(overridden-file)  +
        HOLD(*YES)             +
        SAVE(*YES)
```

- To specify a spooled file name that will identify the report on an output queue (SPLFNAME parameter). This parameter is commonly used to further identify reports printed using the IBM-supplied QSYSPRT and QPRINT printer files.

```
OVRPRTF FILE(QSYSPRT)               +
        SPLFNAME(spooled-file-name)
```

You should be aware of several rules that are in effect when you use file overrides:

- Overrides are applied only at the current invocation level and at any newly created (i.e., lower) invocation levels. They do not apply to higher invocation levels.

- The system will apply only one override per file at any single invocation level. Subsequent overrides to the same file, at the same invocation level, render previous ones obsolete.

Use SECURE(*YES) to prevent mixing overrides.

- A program at a lower invocation level can perform an override command to a file previously overridden at a higher invocation level. When this occurs, any attributes in effect at the higher level will also be in effect at the lower level. Any additional attributes specified by the lower level override will also be in effect. To prevent this mixture of overrides, use the SECURE parameter:

```
OVRDBF FILE(overridden-file)  +
       SECURE(*YES)
```

- The DLTOVR command will delete overrides that exist only at the same invocation level as the OVRxxx command.

- When an invocation level ends, any overrides that exist at that invocation level are deleted.

- Issuing an invalid override command will not cause an error.

Date Format Conversion

Chapter 17

The CVTDAT (Convert Date) Command

The CVTDAT (Convert Date) command changes the format of a date value in a CL program from one format to another. For example, you can change the system date (in the format determined by the QDATFMT system value) to Julian format (YYDDD) to use in a database. The CVTDAT command can also remove or change the date separators (usually / or -) in a date value. You can also use the CVTDAT command to ensure that a data value is indeed a valid date. CL does not support a DATE data type; you must express date values as character strings.

The CVTDAT command uses the following format:

```
CVTDAT DATE(date-to-convert)    +
       TOVAR(converted-date)    +
       FROMFMT(old-format)      +
       TOFMT(new-format)        +
       TOSEP(separators)
```

You can specify a constant or a variable for the DATE parameter; the TODAT parameter is always the name of a CL variable to contain the converted date value. The TOVAR character variable must be long enough to contain the converted date.

The FROMFMT and TOFMT parameters can be any of the following special values:

*JOB	Determined by DATFMT job attribute (default).
*SYSVAL	Determined by QDATFMT system value.
*MDY	MMDDYY format.
*MDYY	MMDDYYYY format.
*DMY	DDMMYY format.
*DMYY	DDMMYYYY format.
*YMD	YYMMDD format.
*YYMD	YYYYMMDD format.

*CYMD	CYYMMDD format (Century is 0 for 1940-1999 and 1 for 2000-2039).
*JUL	YYDDD (Julian format. DDD is 1-366).
*ISO	YYYY-MM-DD (International Organization for Standardization format).
*USA	MM/DD/YYYY format.
*EUR	DD.MM.YYYY (European format).
*JIS	YYYY-MM-DD (Japanese format).

The TOSEP parameter determines the type of separators to be used in the converted date to separate the parts of the date. The parameter value can be a valid separator character (slash (/), hyphen (-), period (.), or comma (,)) or one of the following special values:

*JOB	Determined by DATSEP job attribute (default).
*SYSVAL	Determined by QDATSEP SYSTEM VALUE.
*NONE	Converted date contains no separators.
*BLANK	Blanks are used as separators.

Using CVTDAT To Validate Dates

In addition to using the CVTDAT command to convert date formats, you can use it to determine whether or not a value is a valid date. The following example program receives an 8-character date value in *JOB format. If the date is not valid, the program returns an error indicator to the calling program; it also sends a diagnostic message to the calling program. The error indicator is the message identifier of the diagnostic message.

```
PGM      PARM(&$date &$error)
DCL      &$date    *CHAR 8
DCL      &$error   *CHAR 7
DCL      &$msgf    *CHAR 10
DCL      &$msgflib *CHAR 10

CHGVAR &$error ' '

CVTDAT DATE(&$date) TOVAR(&$date)
MONMSG CPF0500 EXEC(DO)
         RCVMSG      MSGTYPE(*EXCP)               +
                     RMV(*YES)                    +
                     MSGID(&$error)               +
                     MSGF(&$msgf)                 +
                     SNDMSGFLIB(&$msgflib)
         SNDPGMMSG   MSGID(&$error)               +
                     MSGF(&$msgflib/&$msgf)       +
                     MSGTYPE(*DIAG)
         ENDDO
```

```
RETURN
ENDPGM
```

The error indicator and diagnostic message will be one of the following (usually CPF0555):

CPF0550	Date too short for specified format.
CPF0551	Separators in date are not valid.
CPF0552	Date contains misplaced or extra separators.
CPF0553	Date contains too many or too few numeric characters.
CPF0554	Variable specified too short for converted date format.
CPF0555	Date not in specified format or date not valid.
CPF0556	Date contains two or more kinds of separators.
CPF0557	Date outside allowed range.

Using a Message Monitor

Chapter 18

The MONMSG (Monitor Message) Command

There may be occasions when a CL program cannot successfully execute some or all of the commands contained within the program. The result is a program error. If an error condition occurs during execution of a CL program, an escape message is automatically sent to the program. The escape message will identify the error that occurred.

*MONMSG detects
*ESCAPE, *STATUS, and
NOTIFY messages.

To detect when an escape message has been sent to a program, use the MONMSG (Monitor Message) command, which monitors for the arrival of an escape message within a program and allows you to take the appropriate action within the program. The MONMSG command can detect only escape, status, and notify messages; it cannot detect diagnostic or completion messages.

If an error occurs, and you do not monitor for the escape message, the Program Messages display appears; or in the case of a batch job, the system operator receives an inquiry message and must supply the correct reply.

The MONMSG command takes the following form:

```
MONMSG   MSGID(message-identifier)   +
         CMPDTA(comparison-data)     +
         EXEC(CL-command)
```

You cannot specify variables for any of the MONMSG parameter values. The required MSGID parameter specifies the message identifier(s) of up to 50 messages you want to monitor for. You can also monitor for a range of messages instead of specific messages. The following code would monitor for all messages in the CPF9800 range (i.e., all messages from CPF9801 through CPF9899):

```
MONMSG MSGID(CPF9800) EXEC(DO)
         .
         .
         .
       ENDDO
```

To monitor for *all* CPF messages, you would specify CPF0000.

The optional, and rarely used, CMPDTA parameter specifies any comparison data. The default value, which is almost always used, is *NONE (For an explanation of one situation that might warrant using the CMPDTA parameter, see *Using Command Prompting in a CL Program*, page 29). The optional EXEC parameter specifies a single CL command to be executed if the message specified on the MSGID parameter is received. If you do not specify a command for the EXEC parameter, the message(s) will be ignored.

A command-level MONMSG immediately follows a command.

To monitor for messages generated by a single command (i.e., at the command level), the MONMSG command must immediately follow the command. The following code shows how you might use a command-level message monitor. The code uses the CHKOBJ (Check Object) command to check for the existence of a work file in QTEMP; if the file is not found, the program will create the file using the CRTPF (Create Physical File) command.

```
CHKOBJ QTEMP/TEMPWORK *FILE
MONMSG MSGID(CPF9801) EXEC(DO)            +
          CRTPF QTEMP/TEMPWORK RECL(80))
          ENDDO
```

After the command specified on the EXEC parameter is executed, the program continues with the next command in sequence. If the EXEC parameter contains the DO command, the code within the DO loop is executed. If the EXEC parameter contains a GOTO command, control is passed to the command specified at that label. If the command specified on the EXEC parameter is the RETURN command, the program ends normally.

A command-level MONMSG is in effect only for the *single* command that immediately precedes it. A single command can, however, be associated with more than one MONMSG command following it, as long as there are no other intervening commands.

A global MONMSG precedes any executable commands.

A program-level MONMSG (sometimes called a global message monitor) allows you to use just one MONMSG command to monitor for error messages generated by all commands within a CL program. Instead of placing a MONMSG command after each command in your CL program, you can specify just one MONMSG command *before* the first executable command within your program (right after the declarations):

```
MONMSG  MSGID(CPF0000)   +
          EXEC(GOTO ERROR)
```

The EXEC parameter of a program-level MONMSG command, if it is used, *must* specify a GOTO command. No other command can be used with the EXEC parameter at the program level. In the above example, the program would branch to the ERROR label for any unmonitored messages.

If the EXEC parameter is omitted, all errors within the program will be ignored. It is seldom reasonable to ignore all error messages within a program. Usually, you will use a program-level MONMSG command in connection with a generic standard error-handling subroutine. For an example of such a routine, see *A CL Standard Error-Handling Routine,* page 55.

Some programmers prefer to monitor for CPF9999 (Function check) instead of the generic CPF0000 for the program-level monitor. CPF9999 will always occur for an unmonitored message, and has the added advantage of ensuring that all preceding diagnostic messages will be sent before the program sends its final escape message and ends.

You can include command-level MONMSG commands in a program that has a program-level MONMSG command. The program will use the command-level MONMSG before it resorts to the program-level MONMSG.

Sending and Receiving Messages

Chapter 19

Four Major CL Message Commands

Four major CL commands are used to send messages:

- SNDMSG (Send Message)
- SNDBRKMSG (Send Break Message)
- SNDPGMMSG (Send Program Message)
- SNDUSRMSG (Send User Message

It is sometimes difficult to decide which command to use under which circumstances. The following table should help:

	SNDMSG	SNDBRKMSG	SNDPGMMSG	SNDUSRMSG
Allowed at a command line	Yes	Yes	No	No
Allowed in a CL program	Yes	Yes	Yes	Yes
Impromptu MSG allowed	Yes	Yes	Yes	Yes
Predefined MSGID allowed	No	No	Yes	Yes
MSGTYPE(*COMP) allowed	No	No	Yes	Yes
MSGTYPE(*DIAG) allowed	No	No	Yes	No
MSGTYPE(*ESCAPE) allowed	No	No	Yes	No
MSGTYPE(*INFO) allowed	Yes	Yes	Yes	Yes
MSGTYPE(*INQ) allowed	Yes	Yes	Yes	Yes
MSGTYPE(*NOTIFY) allowed	No	No	Yes	No
MSGTYPE(*RQS) allowed	No	No	Yes	No

	SNDMSG	SNDBRKMSG	SNDPGMMSG	SNDUSRMSG
MSGTYPE (*STATUS) allowed	No	No	Yes	No
TOUSR(*SYSOPR) allowed	Yes	No	No	Yes
TOUSR(*ALLACT) allowed	Yes	No	No	No
TOUSR(*REQUESTER) allowed	Yes	No	No	Yes
TOUSR(user) allowed	Yes	No	Yes	Yes
TOMSGQ(*SYSOPR) allowed	Yes	No	Yes	Yes
TOMSGQ(*ALLWS) allowed	No	Yes	No	No
TOMSGQ(QHST) allowed	Yes	No	No	No
TOMSGQ(*) allowed	No	No	No	Yes
TOMSGQ(*EXT) allowed	No	No	No [1]	Yes
TOMSGQ(user) allowed	Yes	No	Yes	Yes
TOMSGQ(workstn) allowed	Yes	Yes	Yes	Yes
TOMSGQ(*TOPGMQ) allowed	No	No	Yes	No
MSGRPY variable allowed	No	No	No	Yes
RPYMSGQ allowed	Yes	Yes	Yes	No

[1] SNDPGMMSG does allow the TOMSGQ(*TOPGMQ) TOPGMQ(*EXT) combination.

Types of Messages

Chapter 20

Rules for Sending and Receiving Messages

A CL program can send and receive several message types; for example, *DIAG, *COMP, *INFO, *INQ, and *ESCAPE. Each message type has a unique purpose; the message type sent will depend on the purpose of the message as determined by the message sender.

Type	Description	Purpose
*COMP	Completion	Signals the successful completion of a processing step.
*DIAG	Diagnostic	Indicates that an error condition exists.
*ESCAPE	Escape	Indicates that a severe error has occurred and that the program that sent the message has ended in error. A program that sends an *ESCAPE message ends immediately.
*INFO	Informational	Informs the recipient of any pertinent information. Not generally used to indicate an error.
*INQ	Inquiry	Requests additional information, which is sent back with a *RPY message.
*NOTIFY	Notification	Can be used as an *INQ or *ESCAPE message, depending on the recipient.

Type	Description	Purpose
*RPY	Reply	Replies to an *INQ or *NOTIFY message.
*RQS	Request	Sends a processing request (i.e., executes a command).
*STATUS	Status	Advises an interactive user of a job's progress. Can also function as an *ESCAPE message.

Consider the following rules about sending and receiving different types of messages:

- A CL program can send any of the message types.
- *INFO, *INQ, and *RPY message types can be sent by a workstation user; all other message types cannot.
- Only *INFO, *INQ, *COMP, and *DIAG message types can be sent to a user message queue, a workstation message queue, or the QSYSOPR message queue.
- All message types except *INQ can be sent to a program message queue.
- All message types except *ESCAPE messages can be sent to the job's external message queue.

The RCVMSG (Receive Message) command can return the message type into a CL variable. For example, the following command receives a message, and places a code indicating the type of message into a CL variable named &$rtntype (*CHAR 2).

```
RCVMSG MSGQ(&$msgqlib/&$msgq)                    +
       MSGKEY(&$msgkey)                          +
       RMV(*NO)                                  +
       MSG(&$msg)                                +
       MSGID(&$msgid)                            +
       RTNTYPE(&$rtntype)
```

The following code identifies the code for each message type. You can include this code in the declarations section of a CL program that will use the RCVMSG command:

```
DCL &$msg_comp *CHAR 2 VALUE('01') /* *COMP                */
DCL &$msg_diag *CHAR 2 VALUE('02') /* *DIAG                */
DCL &$msg_info *CHAR 2 VALUE('04') /* *INFO                */
DCL &$msg_inqy *CHAR 2 VALUE('05') /* *INQ                 */
DCL &$msg_copy *CHAR 2 VALUE('06') /* Copy of *INQ         */
DCL &$msg_reqs *CHAR 2 VALUE('08') /* *RQS                 */
DCL &$msg_reqp *CHAR 2 VALUE('10') /* *RQS w/prompting     */
DCL &$msg_notf *CHAR 2 VALUE('14') /* *NOTIFY              */
DCL &$msg_escp *CHAR 2 VALUE('15') /* *ESCAPE              */
DCL &$msg_rpyn *CHAR 2 VALUE('21') /* *RPY no valid chk    */
DCL &$msg_rpyv *CHAR 2 VALUE('22') /* *RPY w/validity ch   */
DCL &$msg_rpyd *CHAR 2 VALUE('23') /* Default *RPY         */
DCL &$msg_rpys *CHAR 2 VALUE('24') /* Sys default *RPY     */
DCL &$msg_rpyl *CHAR 2 VALUE('25') /* SYSRPYLE *RPY        */
```

See *Using Break-Message-Handling Programs* on page 57 for an example of using these definitions.

A CL Standard Error-Handling Routine

Chapter 21

Global Error Handling

Although you can specify a command-level MONMSG to monitor for messages that can occur during the execution of commands in a CL program, it's unlikely that you can monitor for every possible message that can occur. You should restrict the command-level MONMSG to those errors that you expect could happen during the normal course of using the program. The *CL Command Summary* section of this guide, which starts on page 107, lists the messages that can be monitored for many commands.

You can use a global standard error-handling routine to "gracefully" handle most types of "unexpected" errors that can occur during the execution of the program. When an otherwise unmonitored message occurs, this code will pass the resulting escape message back up the program stack to the calling program, along with any diagnostic messages that preceded it. This technique works the same way that most IBM commands handle errors.

Use this routine with interactive programs.

This standard error-handling routine works best with interactive programs. For batch programs, it is often advantageous to leave out any standard error-handling code and let the system send messages of unexpected errors to the system operator.

Include the following code immediately after the existing declarations section of the CL program:

```
/* Standard error handling declarations */
DCL        &$errorsw *LGL
DCL        &$msgdta  *CHAR 100
DCL        &$msgf    *CHAR 10
DCL        &$msgflib *CHAR 10
DCL        &$msgid   *CHAR 7
DCL        &$msgkey  *CHAR 4

MONMSG     CPF0000 EXEC(GOTO ERROR1)
```

Then continue with the normal processing code for your program. At the end of this processing code, include the following code to complete the program:

```
                RETURN     /* Normal end of program */

                /* Standard error handling routine   */
ERROR1:         IF         &$errorsw                            +
                           (SNDPGMMSG MSGID(CPF9999)            +
                                      MSGF(QCPFMSG)             +
                                      MSGTYPE(*ESCAPE))

                CHGVAR     &$errorsw '1'

ERROR2:         RCVMSG     MSGTYPE(*DIAG))                      +
                           RMV(*NO)                             +
                           KEYVAR(&$msgkey)                     +
                           MSGDTA(&$msgdta)                     +
                           MSGID(&$msgid)                       +
                           MSGF(&$msgf)                         +
                           SNDMSGFLIB(&$msgflib)

                IF         (&$msgkey = ' ')                     +
                           GOTO ERROR3

                RMVMSG     MSGKEY(&$msgkey)

                SNDPGMMSG  MSGID(&$msgid)                       +
                           MSGF(&$msgflib/&$msgf)               +
                           MSGDTA(&$msgdta)                     +
                           MSGTYPE(*DIAG)

                GOTO       ERROR2

ERROR3:         RCVMSG     MSGTYPE(*EXCP)                       +
                           MSGDTA(&$msgdta)                     +
                           MSGID(&$msgid)                       +
                           MSGF(&$msgf)                         +
                           SNDMSGFLIB(&$msgflib)
                SNDPGMMSG  MSGID(&$msgid)
                           MSGF(&$msgflib/&$msgf)               +
                           MSGDTA(&$msgdta)                     +
                           MSGTYPE(*ESCAPE)

                ENDPGM
```

Some programmers prefer to monitor for CPF9999 (Function check) instead of the generic CPF0000 for the program-level monitor. CPF9999 will always occur for an unmonitored message, and has the added advantage of ensuring that all preceding diagnostic messages will be sent before the program sends its final escape message and ends.

Using Break-Message-Handling Programs

Chapter 22

How Break-Handling Programs Work

A break-handling program processes messages arriving at a message queue in *BREAK mode. IBM supplies a default break-handling program: the same command processing program used by the DSPMSG (Display Messages) command. But you can write your own break-handling program if you want break messages to do more than just interrupt your normal work with the Display Messages screen.

A break handler is very versatile. It can process any type of message, such as a completion message or an informational message. It can send customized replies for inquiry messages, it can convert messages to status messages, it can process command request messages, it can initiate a conversational mode of messaging between workstations, and it can redirect messages to another message queue — any number of functions.

Break-handling program requirements.

Remember the following considerations when using a break-handling program:

- A break handler interrupts the job in which the message occurs and processes the message; it then returns control to the job.

- To turn control of message processing over to a break-handling program, use the following CL command:

```
CHGMSGQ   MSGQ(msgq_name)     +
          DLVRY(*BREAK)       +
          PGM(program_name)   +
          SEV(severity_code)
```

- OS/400 calls the break handler if a message of high enough severity reaches the message queue. If you use a break handler in a job that is already using the system reply list, the reply list will get control of the messages first.

- A break-handling program must accept three arguments from OS/400: (1) the name of the message queue, (2) the name of the library containing the message queue, and (3) the reference key of the received message.

- The break handler must receive the reference message, usually using the RCVMSG (Receive Message) CL command.

This break handler converts messages to status messages.

The following brief program is a sample break handler. It displays any notify or inquiry messages, along with some Office messages or messages indicating severe conditions, such as DASD problems. It converts other messages to status messages, so that they appear at the bottom of a user's screen without interrupting work.

```
PGM        PARM(&$msgq &$msgqlib &$msgkey)

DCL        &$msgq        *CHAR 10
DCL        &$msgqlib     *CHAR 10
DCL        &$msgkey      *CHAR 4
DCL        &$msg         *CHAR 132
DCL        &$msgid       *CHAR 7
DCL        &$rtntype     *CHAR 2
DCL        &$msg_inqy    *CHAR 2    VALUE('05') /* *INQ    */
DCL        &$msg_notf    *CHAR 2    VALUE('14') /* *NOTIFY */

MONMSG     CPF0000 EXEC(GOTO ERROR)

/* Receive message                                          */
RCVMSG     MSGQ(&$msgqlib/&$msgq)                           +
           MSGKEY(&$msgkey)                                 +
           RMV(*NO)                                         +
           MSG(&$msg)                                       +
           MSGID(&$msgid)                                   +
           RTNTYPE(&$rtntype)

/* Display *INQ, *NOTIFY messages.                          */
/* Also display Office, serious condition messages.         */
   IF      ((&$rtntype *EQ &$msg_inqy) *OR                  +
            (&$rtntype *EQ &$msg_notf) *OR                  +
            (&$msgid *EQ 'OFC0089') *OR                     +
            (&$msgid *EQ 'OFC0090') *OR                     +
            (&$msgid *EQ 'OFC0091'))                        +
           DO
           DSPMSG MSGQ(&$msgqlib/&$msgq)
           ENDDO

/* Resend other messages as *STATUS messages               */
   ELSE    DO
           SNDPGMMSG MSGID(CPI2401)                         +
                     MSGF(QCPFMSG)                          +
                     MSGDTA(&$msg)                          +
                     TOPGMQ(*EXT)                           +
                     MSGTYPE(*STATUS)
           ENDDO
RETURN

/* Error handling                                           */
ERROR:
   SNDPGMMSG MSGID(CPI2401)                                 +
             MSGF(QCPFMSG)                                  +
             MSGDTA('Break handling program failed.)        +
```

```
                         TOMSGQ(*SYSOPR)                        +
                         MSGTYPE(*ESCAPE)
             RETURN
             ENDPGM
```

Processing Outfiles

Chapter 23

Commands that Offer Outfiles

Some IBM-supplied commands offer the ability to place the results of the command in a database file called an *outfile* instead of displaying or printing the results. You can then further process the information in the outfile to perform actions that aren't otherwise provided by the system. Frequently used commands that offer outfiles are

DSPAUTL (Display Authorization List)
DSPAUTLOBJ (Display Authorization List Objects)
DSPBNDDIR (Display Binding Directory)
DSPDBR (Display Database Relations)
DSPDIR (Display Directory)
DSPFD (Display File Description)
DSPFFD (Display File Field Descriptions)
DSPMOD (Display Module)
DSPOBJAUT (Display Object Authority)
DSPOBJD (Display Object Description)
DSPPGMADP (Display Programs That Adopt)
DSPPGMREF (Display Program References)
DSPUSRPRF (Display User Profile)
RSTCFG (Restore Configuration)
RSTDLO (Restore Document Library Object)
RSTLIB (Restore Library)
RSTOBJ (Restore Object)
RSTUSRPRF (Restore User Profile)
SAVCFG (Save Configuration)
SAVCHGOBJ (Save Changed Object)
SAVDLO (Save Document Library Object)
SAVLIB (Save Library)
SAVOBJ (Save Object)
SAVSAVFDTA (Save Save File Data)
SAVSECDTA (Save Security Data)
SAVSYS (Save System)

IBM supplies models of the outfiles that it supports. You should not place data directly into these models. Instead, use the OVRDBF (Override with Database File) command to redirect the output to another file of your own creation. The *CL Command Summary*, starting on page 107, will give you the names of the outfiles for each covered command.

How To Process an Outfile

The following example code illustrates how to process an outfile in a CL program. You can easily adapt this code to use with any outfile supported by any command. This code segment uses the DSPOBJD (Display Object Description) command to place information about all the objects in library QGPL into an outfile named QADSPOBJ. The code then reads and processes each record in the outfile.

```
          /* Declare appropriate model outfile.              */
          DCLF     QADSPOBJ

          /* Delete outfile in QTEMP if it exists.           */
          DLTF     QTEMP/QADSPOBJ
          MONMSG   CPF2105  EXEC(DO)
                   RCVMSG   MSGTYPE(*EXCP) /* Remove CPF2105. */
                   ENDDO

          /* Execute IBM command to an outfile.              */
          DSPOBJD  OBJ(QGPL/*ALL)                            +
                   OBJTYPE(*ALL)                             +
                   OUTPUT(*OUTFILE)                          +
                   OUTFILE(QTEMP/QADSPOBJ)

          /* Redirect program to use outfile in QTEMP.       */
          OVRDBF   QADSPOBJ                                  +
                   TOFILE(QTEMP/QADSPOBJ)                    +
                   SECURE(*YES)

          /* Read/process records in QTEMP/outfile.          */
LOOP:
          RCVF
          MONMSG   CPF0864  EXEC(DO)        /* End of file.  */
                   RCVMSG   MSGTYPE(*EXCP) /* Remove CPF0864. */
                   GOTO     ENDOFFILE
                   ENDDO
          .
          .   (Process records in outfile.)
          .
          GOTO     LOOP             /* Loop back for next record. */
ENDOFFILE:
```

Retrieving Job Attributes

Chapter 24

The RTVJOBA (Retrieve Job Attributes) Command

The RTVJOBA (Retrieve Job Attributes) command will retrieve the attributes of the current job (i.e., the job in which the command is used), and place the values of those attributes into a CL program variable. The following list shows the attributes you can retrieve, the proper declaration for the CL variable to hold the attribute, and a brief description of the attribute.

ACGCDE	*CHAR 15	Accounting code.
BRKMSG	*CHAR 7	Break message handling mode.
CCSID	*DEC (5 0)	Coded character set identifier.
CNTRYID	*CHAR 2	Country identifier.
CURLIB	*CHAR 10	Current library for job, or *NONE.
CURUSER	*CHAR 10	User profile of the current user.
DATE	*CHAR 6	Job date (DATFMT format).
DATFMT	*CHAR 4	Date format for job.
DATSEP	*CHAR 1	Date separator character for job.
DDMCNV	*CHAR 5	Action taken for DDM conversations.
DEVRCYACN	*CHAR 13	Recovery action for workstation I/O errors on an interactive job.

DFTWAIT	*DEC (7 0)	Default time that system waits for an instruction to be processed (1-9999999 seconds or -1=*NOMAX).
ENDSTS	*CHAR 1	Cancellation status. 1=Controlled cancel in progress, 0=No cancel in progress.
INQMSGRPY	*CHAR 10	Inquiry message handling method.
JOB	*CHAR 10	Job name.
LANGID	*CHAR 3	Language identifier.
LOGLVL	*CHAR 1	Message logging level (0 4).
LOGSEV	*DEC (2 0)	Minimum message logging severity (00-99)
LOGTYPE	*CHAR 10	Job log message text level.
LOGCLPGM	*CHAR 10	Log CL commands in job log.
NBR	*CHAR 6	Job number.
OUTQ	*CHAR 10	Output queue used for spooled output.
OUTQLIB	*CHAR 10	Library for OUTQ.
PRTDEV	*CHAR 10	Printer device.
PRTKEYFMT	*CHAR 10	Print key format (*NONE, *PRTBDR, *PRTHDR, or *PRTALL).
PRTTXT	*CHAR 30	Print text.
PURGE	*CHAR 10	Eligible for main storage purge at end of timeslice or long wait.
RTNCDE	*DEC (5 0)	Completion status code of last program in job. 0=Normal return, 1=Returned with RPG LR on, 2=Error, 3=Halt indicator set.
RUNPTY	*DEC (2 0)	Processing priority (1-99).
SBMMSGQ	*CHAR 10	Message queue.
SBMMSGQLIB	*CHAR 10	Library for SBMMSGQ.

SRTSEQ	*CHAR 10	Name of sort sequence table, or *LANGIDUNQ, *LANGIDSHR, or *HEX.
SRTSEQLIB	*CHAR 10	Library for SRTSEQ.
STSMSG	*CHAR 7	Status message handling method.
SUBTYPE	*CHAR 1	Job environment subtype. *=No subtype, E=Evoked, T=Multiple Requester Terminal (MRT), J=Prestart, P=Print driver.
SWS	*CHAR 8	Job switch values (0 or 1).
SYSLIBL	*CHAR 165	System portion of library list (up to 15 11-character fields, blank padded).
TIMSEP	*CHAR 1	Time separator character for job.
TIMESLICE	*DEC (7 0)	Job's timeslice (1-9999999 milliseconds).
TSEPOOL	*CHAR 10	Value indicating whether interactive jobs move to another main storage pool at end of timeslice.
TYPE	*CHAR 1	Job environment. 0=Batch job, 1=Interactive job.
USER	*CHAR 10	User profile associated with the job.
USRLIBL	*CHAR 275	User portion of library list (up to 25 11-character fields, blank padded).

For example, to retrieve the name of the current job, and build a string containing the qualified name, a CL program would include the following code:

```
DCL   &$nbr          *CHAR 6
      DCL   &$user    *CHAR 10
      DCL   &$job     *CHAR 10
      DCL   &$qualjob *CHAR 28
      .
      .
      .
      RTVJOBA    NBR(&$nbr)            +
                 USER(&$user)          +
                 JOB(&$job)
      CHGVAR     &$qualjob            +
                 (&$nbr   *CAT '/' *CAT +
                  &$user *CAT '/' *CAT +
                  &$job)
```

The qualified job name would then be in variable &$qualjob.

Retrieving Object Descriptions

Chapter 25

The RTVOBJD (Retrieve Object Description) Command

The RTVOBJD (Retrieve Object Description) command will retrieve the attributes of a specific object and place the values of those attributes into a CL program variable. The following list shows the attributes you can retrieve, the proper declaration for the CL variable to hold the attribute, and a brief description of the attribute:

ALWAPICHG	*CHAR 1	Allow change by program flag. '0'=Cannot change with QLICOBJD (Change Object Description) API, '1'=Change allowed with QLICOBJD.
APAR	*CHAR 10	APAR (Problem report) ID that caused this object to be patched.
APICHG	*CHAR 1	Object changed by QLICOBJD. '0'=Not changed, '1'=Changed.
ASP	*DEC (2 0)	Auxiliary storage pool ID. 1=System ASP, 2-16=User ASPs.
CHGDATE	*CHAR 13	Last change date and time (CYYMMDDHHMMSS or blank).
COMPILER	*CHAR 16	Compiler identifier and level at creation (5738xxxVxxRxxMxx, where 5738xxx=Compiler,

			Vxx=Version, Rxx=Release, Mxx=Modification level).
CPR	*CHAR 1		Compression status. Y=Compressed, N=Not compressed, T=Temporarily decompressed, F=Saved with STG(*FREE), X=Ineligible for compression.
CRTDATE	*CHAR 13		Object creation date and time (CYYMMDDHHMMSS).
CRTSYSTEM	*CHAR 8		Name of the system on which the object was created.
CRTUSER	*CHAR 10		User profile of the user who created the object.
LICPGM	*CHAR 16		For licensed programs, the licensed program identifier and level (5738xxxVxxRxxMxx, where 5738xxx=Licensed program, Vxx=Version, Rxx=Release, Mxx=Modification level).
OBJATR	*CHAR 10		Extended attribute, e.g., program or file type.
OBJAUD	*CHAR 10		Auditing value (*NONE, *USRPRF, *CHANGE, or *ALL).
OBJDMN	*CHAR 2		Object domain. *U=User domain, *S=System domain.
OBJLVL	*CHAR 8		Object control level.
OVFASP	*CHAR 1		Object overflowed ASP flag. 0=Object did not overflow, 1=Object overflowed ASP.
OWNER	*CHAR 10		User profile of the owner.
PTF	*CHAR 10		Program Temporary Fix number.

RESETDATE	*CHAR 7	Date USEDATE last updated (CYYMMDD or blanks).
RSTDATE	*CHAR 13	Last restore date and time (CYYMMDDHHMMSS or blank).
RTNLIB	*CHAR 10	Name of the library that contains the object.
SAVACTDATE	*CHAR 13	Last save-while-active date and time (CYYMMDDHHMMSS or blank).
SAVCMD	*CHAR 10	Last save command used.
SAVDATE	*CHAR 13	Last save date and time (CYYMMDDHHMMSS or blank).
SAVDEV	*CHAR 10	Last save device type. *SAVF=Save file, *DKT=Diskette, *TAP=Tape.
SAVF	*CHAR 10	Last save file, if SAVDEV=*SAVF.
SAVFLIB	*CHAR 10	Last save file library, if SAVDEV=*SAVF.
SAVLABEL	*CHAR 17	File label of last save to tape or diskette.
SAVSIZE	*DEC (15 0)	Object size when last saved (bytes).
SAVSEQNBR	*DEC (4 0)	Last save tape sequence number.
SAVVOL	*CHAR 71	Last save tape or diskette volume(s). Up to 10 six-character volumes, each followed by a blank. If more than 10 volumes, position 71 contains a '1'.
SIZE	*DEC (15 0)	Object size (bytes).
SRCDATE	*CHAR 13	Source date and time (CYYMMDDHHMMSS).
SRCF	*CHAR 10	Source file used to create object.
SRCFLIB	*CHAR 10	Source file library.

SRCMBR	*CHAR 10	Source member.
STG	*CHAR 10	Storage status. *FREE=Data freed and object suspended, *KEEP=Date not freed and object not suspended.
SYSLVL	*CHAR 9	Operating system level at creation (VxxRxxMxx, where Vxx=Version, Rxx=Release, Mxx=Modification level).
TEXT	*CHAR 50	Descriptive text.
USECOUNT	*DEC (5 0)	Number of days used (0 if USEDATE=0).
USEDATE	*CHAR 7	Date of last use (CYYMMDD, or blank if USEUPD=N).
USEUPD	*CHAR 1	Usage update flag. Y=Usage is logged, N=Usage is not logged.
USRCHG	*CHAR 1	Program modified by user flag. '0'=Not modified, '1'=Modified by user.
USRDFNATR	*CHAR 10	User-defined attribute, if any.

For example, to retrieve the date last changed and the date last saved for program object QGPL/QDCUPF, a CL program would include the following code:

```
DCL        &$chgdate *CHAR 13
DCL        &$savdate *CHAR 13
.
.
.

RTVOBJD    OBJ(QGPL/QDCUPF)      +
           OBJTYPE(*PGM)         +
           CHGDATE(&$chgdate)    +
           SAVDATE(&$savdate)
```

The CL variables &$chgdate and &$savdate would then contain the change date and save date, respectively.

Retrieving Member Descriptions

Chapter 26

The RTVMBRD (Retrieve Member Description) Command

The RTVMBRD (Retrieve Member Description) command will retrieve the attributes of a specific file member, and place the values of those attributes into a CL program variable. The following list shows the attributes you can retrieve, the proper declaration for the CL variable to hold the attribute, and a brief description of the attribute:

ACCPTHSIZ	*DEC (12 0)	Access path size, in bytes.
CHGDATE	*CHAR 13	Date/time the member was last changed (CYYMMDDHHMMSS).
CRTDATE	*CHAR 13	Date/time the member was created (CYYMMDDHHMMSS).
DTASPCSIZ	*DEC (15 0)	Data space size of member, in bytes.
EXPDATE	*CHAR 7	Member expiration date (CYYMMDD).
FILEATR	*CHAR 3	File attribute. *PF=physical file, *LF=logical file.
FILETYPE	*CHAR 5	File type. *DATA=data member, *SRC=source member.
NBRCURRCD	*DEC(10 0)	Number of nondeleted records in member.
NBRDLTRCD	*DEC (10 0)	Number of deleted records in member.

NBRDTAMBRS	*DEC (2 0)	Number of data members for a logical file member.
RESETDATE	*CHAR 7	Date the USEDATE count was reset (CYYMMDD).
RSTDATE	*CHAR 13	Date/time the member was restored (CYYMMDDHHMMSS).
RTNLIB	*CHAR 10	Name of the library that contains the file.
RTNMBR	*CHAR 10	Member name.
RTNSYSTEM	*CHAR 4	System indicator from where the description was retrieved. *LCL=local system, *RMT=remote system.
SAVDATE	*CHAR 13	Date/time the member was last saved (CYYMMDDHHMMSS).
SHARE	*CHAR 4	Shared open data path: *YES, *NO.
SRCCHGDATE	*CHAR 13	Date/time the source member was last changed (CYYMMDDHHMMSS).
SRCTYPE	*CHAR 10	Source type. RPG=RPG source, CLP=CL program source, ...
TEXT	*CHAR 50	Member text.
USECOUNT	*DEC (5 0)	Number of days the member has been used.
USEDATE	*CHAR 7	Date the member was last used (CYYMMDD).

Retrieving User Profiles

Chapter 27

The RTVUSRPRF (Retrieve User Profile) Command

The RTVUSRPRF (Retrieve User Profile) command will retrieve the attributes of a specific user profile, and place the values of those attributes into a CL program variable. The following list shows the attributes you can retrieve, the proper declaration for the CL variable to hold the attribute, and a brief description of the attribute:

ACGCDE	*CHAR 15	Accounting code.
ASTLVL	*CHAR 10	Assistance level: *SYSVAL, *BASIC, *INTERMED, *ADVANCED.
ATNPGM	*CHAR 10	Default attention key handling program: name, *SYSVAL, *NONE.
ATNPGMLIB	*CHAR 10	Attention key program library.
AUDLVL	*CHAR 640	Object auditing level entries (up to 64).
CCSID	*DEC (5 0)	Coded character set identifier: identifier, -2 = *SYSVAL.
CNTRYID	*CHAR 10	Country identifier: identifier, *SYSVAL.
CURLIB	*CHAR 10	Current library: name, *CRTDFT.
DLVRY	*CHAR 10	Message control delivery value: *NOTIFY, *BREAK, *HOLD, *DFT.
DSPSGNINF	*CHAR 7	Display sign-on information display: *SYSVAL, *YES, *NO.

GRPPRF	*CHAR 10	Group profile, or *NONE.	
GRPAUT	*CHAR 10	Authority granted to group profile for created objects: *NONE, *CHANGE, *ALL, *USE, *EXCLUDE.	
INLMNU	*CHAR 10	Initial menu when user signs on.	
INLMNULIB	*CHAR 10	Initial menu library.	
INLPGM	*CHAR 10	Initial program.	
INLPGMLIB	*CHAR 10	Initial program library.	
JOBD	*CHAR 10	User's job description.	
JOBDLIB	*CHAR 10	Job description library.	
KBDBUF	*CHAR 10	Keyboard buffering: *SYSVAL, *NO, *TYPEAHEAD, *YES.	
LMTCPB	*CHAR 10	Limit command capability: *NO, *YES, *PARTIAL.	
LMTDEVSSN	*CHAR 7	Limit device sessions: *SYSVAL, *YES, *NO.	
LANGID	*CHAR 10	Language identifier: identifier, *SYSVAL.	
MAXSTG	*DEC (11 0)	Maximum auxiliary storage space allowed to user, in KB. -1 = *NOMAX.	
MSGQ	*CHAR 10	Message queue.	
MSGQLIB	*CHAR 10	Message queue library.	
NOTVLDSIGN	*DEC (11 0)	Number of invalid sign-on attempts.	
OBJAUD	*CHAR 10	Object auditing value:*NONE, *CHANGE, *ALL.	
OUTQ	*CHAR 10	Output queue: name, *DEV, *WRKSTN.	
OUTQLIB	*CHAR 10	Output queue library.	
OWNER	*CHAR 10	Owner of created objects: *USRPRF or *GRPPRF.	
PRTDEV	*CHAR 10	Default printer device: name, *SYSVAL, *WORKSTN.	

PRVSIGN	*CHAR 13	Previous sign-on date/time (CYYMMDDHHMMSS).
PTYLMT	*CHAR 1	Highest scheduling priority allowed for user (JOBPTY and OUTPTY): 0-9.
PWDCHGDAT	*CHAR 6	Last password change date (YYMMDD).
PWDEXP	*CHAR 4	Password expired: *YES, *NO.
PWDEXPITV	*DEC (5 0)	Password expiration interval (days): 1-366, 0 = *SYSVAL, -1 = *NOMAX.
RTNUSRPRF	*CHAR 10	The name of the user profile retrieved.
SEV	*DEC (2 0)	Message control severity level: 00-99.
SPCAUT	*CHAR 100	List of special user authorities, up to 10, each 10 characters long.
SPCENV	*CHAR 10	Special environment: *SYSVAL, *NONE, *S36.
SRTSEQ	*CHAR 10	Sort sequence table identifier: identifier, *HEX, *LANGIDUNQ, *LANGIDSHR, *SYSVAL.
SRTSEQLIB	*CHAR 10	Sort sequence table library.
STATUS	*CHAR 10	User status: *ENABLED, *DISABLED.
STGUSED	*DEC (15 0)	Auxiliary storage space currently used by user, in KB.
TEXT	*CHAR 50	Text description of user profile.
USRCLS	*CHAR 10	User class: *USER, *SYSOPR, *PGMR, *SECADM, *SECOFR.
USROPT	*CHAR 240	User option values (up to 24).

Retrieving the Name of the Current Program

Chapter 28

The Code You'll Need

Unlike RPG, CL does not provide access to a program status or file information data structure. A CL program, therefore, does not provide a direct method of retrieving the name of the program currently running. You can, however, get the name of the program using the code in this section. Include the following declarations in the CL program:

```
DCL        &$pgm      *CHAR   10
DCL        &$msgkey   *CHAR    4
DCL        &$sender   *CHAR   80
```

To retrieve the program name, placing its value into variable &$pgm, use the following code section:

```
SNDPGMMSG  MSG('Dummy')                   +
           TOPGMQ(*PRV)                    +
           MSGTYPE(*INFO)                  +
           KEYVAR(&$msgkey)
RCVMSG     PGMQ(*PRV)                      +
           MSGKEY(&$msgkey)                +
           RMV(*YES)                       +
           SENDER(&$sender)
CHGVAR     &$pgm %SST(&$sender 56 10)
```

Write your own
RTVCURPGM command.

If you need to retrieve the program name often, you could write a RTVCURPGM (Retrieve Current Program) command. The command source would be

```
CMD   'Retrieve Current Program'
PARM  PGM  *CHAR  10                 +
      RTNVAL(*YES)                   +
      PROMPT('Program name (10)')
PARM  LIB  *CHAR  10                 +
      RTNVAL(*YES)                   +
      PROMPT('Library name (10)')
```

The following source for program RTVCURPGMC constitutes the command processing program:

```
          PGM   (&$pgm &$lib)

          DCL   &$pgm      *CHAR  10
          DCL   &$lib      *CHAR  10
          DCL   &$msgkey   *CHAR   4
          DCL   &$sender   *CHAR  80

          SNDPGMMSG   MSG('Dummy')                 +
                      TOPGMQ(*PRV)                  +
                      MSGTYPE(*INFO)                +
                      KEYVAR(&$msgkey)
          RCVMSG      PGMQ(*PRV)                    +
                      MSGKEY(&$msgkey)              +
                      RMV(*YES)                     +
                      SENDER(&$sender)
          CHGVAR      &$pgm %SST(&$sender 56 10)

          RTVOBJD     &$pgm                         +
                      OBJTYPE(*PGM)                 +
                      RTNLIB(&$lib)
          MONMSG      CPF0000 EXEC(DO)
                      CHGVAR &$lib '*UNKNOWN'
                      ENDDO

       ENDPGM
```

Use the CRTCLPGM and CRTCMD commands to create these objects. Since the command uses return variables, you should specify ALLOW(*BPGM *IPGM) on the CRTCMD command, to restrict use to programs.

When you need to use the RTVCURPGM command in a program, use the following code:

```
DCL           &$pgm      *CHAR  10
DCL           &$pgmlib   *CHAR  10
.
.
.
RTVCURPGM   &$pgm &$pgmlib
```

To properly retrieve the program's library name, the program must be in your library list; if the program occurs more than once in your library list, RTVCURPGM will retrieve the name of the first library. If it cannot find the program in the library list, RTVCURPGM will return LIB(*UNKNOWN).

Using OPNQRYF

Chapter 29

The OPNQRYF (Open Query File) Command

The OPNQRYF (Open Query File) command creates an open data path (ODP) to a file to provide an alternate view of the records in a database file. This ODP contains a subset of the database records of the original file and can be arranged in the order you specify. An HLL program can process the records in this ODP, just as if it were processing the file the ODP is based upon — without any modification to the program. The OPNQRYF command is most commonly used to

- Select a subset of available records:

```
OPNQRYF FILE(library/file    +
            member           +
            record-format)   +
      QRYSLT('selection')
```

- Order records by the value of one or more fields in the record:

```
OPNQRYF FILE(library/file        +
            member               +
            record-format)       +
      KEYFLD(file/field          +
            collating-order      +
            absolute-value)
```

OPNQRYF defaults to opening the query file (i.e., the ODP) for input only. You can change this default by specifying an OPTION parameter. The valid OPTION values are *ALL, *INP, *OUT, *UPD, and *DLT.

*OPNQRYF requires shared data paths: SHARE(*YES).*

To use OPNQRYF in a CL program, the file to be queried must specify SHARE(*YES). Usually, you will use the OVRDBF (Override with Database File) command to ensure open data path sharing, as in the following code segment:

```
OVRDBF  FILE(overridden-file)      +
        TOFILE(library/file)       +
        MBR(member)                +
        SHARE(*YES)
OPNQRYF FILE((file member))        +
        QRYSLT('selection')        +
        KEYFLD(file/field          +
               collating-order     +
               absolute-value)
```

The QRYSLT parameter is similar to SQL.

The QRYSLT parameter determines which records will be included in the query file. Its syntax is similar in some respects to that of Structured Query Language (SQL). To select all records in a file, use QRYSLT(*ALL). To add flexibility to OPNQRYF in your CL programs, consider using a CL variable in place of the QRYSLT string. Using the CHGVAR command, you can build the QRYSLT string to meet different needs. Or you can pass the QRYSLT string to the CL program as a parameter. (If the string is longer than 32 bytes, see *Passing Constant Parameters Between Programs*, page 23, for important information.) Use the following sample program as the basis for using this technique. This code accepts beginning and ending ZIP Codes as parameters, then builds a QRYSLT string to select records in the requested ZIP Code range.

```
        PGM     PARM(&fromzip &tozip)


        DCL     &fromzip    *CHAR 5
        DCL     &tozip      *CHAR 5
        DCL     &qryslt     *CHAR 512

/* Build QRYSLT string: 'ZIPCODE = %RANGE("xxxxx" "xxxxx")' */
/*                 or: '*ALL'                                */

        IF      (&fromzip *NE '*ALL') DO
                CHGVAR &qryslt                          +
                       ('ZIPCODE = %RANGE("' *CAT       +
                       &fromzip *CAT '" "' *CAT         +
                       &tozip *CAT '")')
                ENDDO
        ELSE    DO
                CHGVAR &qryslt ('*ALL')
                ENDDO

/* Perform file override to SHARE(*YES                      */
        OVRDBF  MAILMAST SHARE(*YES)

/* Execute OPNQRYF  command                                 */
        OPNQRYF FILE(MAILLIST)                          +
                QRYSLT(&qryslt)                         +
                KEYFLD((COUNTRY) (ZIPCODE *DESCEND))

/* Call high level language processing program             */
        CALL    PRINTLABEL

/* Close files, delete overrides                           */
        CLOF
        DLTOVR  FILE(*ALL)
```

```
                       RETURN
                       ENDPGM
```

Use CPYFRMQRYF to create a copy of the OPNQRYF results.

CL cannot process an OPNQRYF open data path. You must use a high-level language (HLL) to actually process the data in the query file. Also, the query file exists only within the job that created it. To allow CL to process the data in the query file, or to make the ODP a permanent object on your system, use the CPYFRMQRYF (Copy from Query File) command:

```
CPYFRMQYRF FROMOPNID(file)                      +
             TOFILE(library/file)               +
             TOMBR(member)                       +
             MBROPT(*NONE|*ADD|*REPLACE)         +
             CRTFILE(*NO|*YES)
```

Remember that the copy that CPYFRMQRYF makes will not reflect any new changes made in the original file after the CPYFRMQRYF completes.

OPNQRYF supports a rich expression syntax. In many ways, the expressions on the QRYSLT parameter (along with the GRPSLT and MAPFLD parameters) are similar to CL expressions, but there are some differences:

- Database field names do not require a leading ampersand (&).

- OPNQRYF supports additional data types, including floating-point and date types.

- OPNQRYF does *not* support *BCAT and *TCAT.

- OPNQRYF supports nested functions.

- OPNQRYF supports many more built-in functions and operators than does CL, including trignonometric, data arithmetic, square root, and statistical functions.

Using CL's Built-In SQL Functions

Chapter 30

Query Management

Structured Query Language (SQL) is a standard syntax used to retrieve information from a database file. SQL/400 is a licensed program product on the AS/400, offered separately from the OS/400 operating system. But the "engine" that runs SQL is built into the operating system, and you can make use of it without licensing the SQL/400 product. The OS/400 function is called Query Management.

The following commands relate to Query Management:

- CRTQMQRY (Create Query Management Query)
- DLTQMQRY (Delete Query Management Query)
- RTVQMQRY (Retrieve Query Management Query)
- STRQMQRY (Start Query Management Query)
- WRKQMQRY (Work with Query Management Queries)

*QMQRY source is a single SQL statement.

CRTQMQRY creates a Query Management query (AS/400 object type *QMQRY) from a source member (SEU type QMQRY). The source is a single SQL statement, which may span several records in the source member. It can include up to 50 variable substitution values (up to 55 characters each) and comments. The following example would be a valid source statement for a Query Management Query:

```
SELECT * FROM QADSPOBJ WHERE ODOBTP="&sqlvar1"
```

STRQMQRY command executes a *QMQRY object. You can display or print the resulting output from the SQL query, or you can store it in an outfile (OUTPUT parameter). If the query contains substitution variables, you can assign values for the variables (SETVAR parameter). You can run the query against the local database or a remote one (if you have defined a remote database using the ADDRDBDIRE (Add Relational Database Directory Entry) command). You could execute the example query shown above, with the following command:

```
STRQMQRY QMQRY(query-name)                     +
         SETVAR((SQLVAR1 '*FILE'))
```

All records with field ODOBTP equal to a value of *FILE would be shown.

A *QMQRY object can consist solely of variables.

The SQL statement can consist only of variables, to allow you to specify an SQL statement at the time you run the query. For example, the source could be as follows:

```
&sqlvar1 &sqlvar2
```

After creating the *QMQRY object, you could execute it using the following statement:

```
STRQMQRY QMQRY(query-name)                                +
         SETVAR((SQLVAR1 'select * from qadspobj')  +
                (SQLVAR2 'where odobtp = "*FILE"'))
```

If you have the Query/400 product installed on your AS/400, you can retrieve the appropriate SQL source statement from Query/400's *QRYDFN object. RTVQMQRY will retrieve the source from either a *QMQRY object or a *QRYDFN object.

Processing a Qualified Name

Chapter 31

Qualified Names

CL can process one or more program variables in a qualified name, as long as it declares each qualifier as a separate variable. For example, to act upon a qualified object, a CL program could include the following code:

```
DCL     &$object  *CHAR 10
DCL     &$library *CHAR 10
.
.
CHGVAR  &$object  'QRPGSRC'
CHGVAR  &$library 'QGPL'
WRKOBJ  &$library/&$object
```

CL processes all elements in a qualified name as separate variables.

CL will not allow you to specify the qualified name in one variable. The following example would *not* work:

```
DCL     &$qualobj *CHAR 21
.
.
CHGVAR  &$qualobj 'QGPL/QRPGSRC'
WRKOBJ  &$qualobj
```

The system must view the variable values as two separate entities, not as a single character string.

To process a qualified value in a single character string, you can use the QCMDEXC program. You could modify the above example to use the qualified name in a single string:

```
DCL       &$qualobj *CHAR 21
DCL       &$command *CHAR 28
.
.
.
CHGVAR    &$qualobj 'QGPL/QRPGSRC'
CHGVAR    &$command ('WRKOBJ' *BCAT &$qualobj)
CALL      QCMDEXC PARM(&$command 28)
```

Use this code to process a qualified name passed by a CL command.

CL commands pass qualified command parameters to their command processing program as a single variable. The CPP must break down the parts of the qualified name to process it. In the case of a qualified object name, the variable is 20 characters long, with the object name in the first 10 characters, and the library name in the second 10 characters. The following code will break down a qualified object name in a CL program:

```
PGM       PARM(&$qualobj)
DCL       &$qualobj *CHAR 20
DCL       &$object  *CHAR 10
DCL       &$library *CHAR 10
.
.
.
CHGVAR    &$object  %SST(&$qualobj  1 10)
CHGVAR    &$library %SST(&$qualobj 11 10)
```

CL commands pass a qualified job name as a 26-character variable, with the job name, user profile, and job number. The following code will break down a qualified job name into its components:

```
PGM       PARM(&$qualjob)
DCL       &$qualjob *CHAR 26
DCL       &$jobname *CHAR 10
DCL       &$jobuser *CHAR 10
DCL       &$jobnbr  *CHAR 10
.
.
.
CHGVAR    &$jobname %SST(&$qualjob  1 10)
CHGVAR    &$jobuser %SST(%$qualjob 11 10)
CHGVAR    &$jobnbr  %SST(&$qualjob 21  6)
```

Processing Lists

Chapter 32

List Parameters

Occasionally, it may be necessary to process a list of values in the same parameter. For example, the LIBL parameter of the CHGLIBL (Change Library List) command is a list of libraries. Also, if the CL program is a command processing program that operates with a command that passes list parameters, you will need to know how to process the list.

You can represent each element of a list using individually declared CL variables:

```
DCL       &$lib1   *CHAR 10   VALUE(QTEMP)
DCL       &$lib2   *CHAR 10   VALUE(QGPL)
DCL       &$lib3   *CHAR 10   VALUE(PAYROLL)
.
.
.
CHGLIBL   LIBL(&$lib1 &$lib2 &$lib3)
```

You *cannot*, however, specify all the elements in a list as a single character string. The following code would *not* work:

```
DCL       &$libl   *CHAR 18   VALUE('QTEMP QGPL PAYROLL')
.
.
.
CHGLIBL   LIBL(&$libl)
```

Use %SST and %BIN to process a simple list.

To process a simple list parameter passed by a command, you must use the %SST and %BIN built-in functions to break the parameter down into separate variables. Commands pass simple list parameters in two parts. The first two bytes of the parameter consist of a binary value representing the number of values passed in the list. The rest of the parameter consists of the actual list elements. Commands pass only the number of elements indicated by the first two bytes, and your CL program must process only that number of elements. The following code illustrates how to break down the passed parameter into its individual list elements:

```
PGM        PARM(&$libl)
DCL        &$libl    *CHAR   32
DCL        &$lib1    *CHAR   10
DCL        &$lib2    *CHAR   10
DCL        &$lib3    *CHAR   10
DCL        &$nbr     *DEC    (5 0)
.
.
.
CHGVAR     &$nbr     %BIN(&$libl 1 2)
IF         (&$nbr *GE 1) THEN(CHGVAR   &$lib1   %SST(&$libl  3 10))
IF         (&$nbr *GE 2) THEN(CHGVAR   &$lib2   %SST(&$libl 13 10))
IF         (&$nbr *GE 3) THEN(CHGVAR   &$lib3   %SST(&$libl 23 10))
```

You can also process successive elements of a list parameter using a similar technique:

```
PGM        PARM(&$libl)
DCL        &$libl     *CHAR   32
DCL        &$lible    *CHAR   10
DCL        &$nbr      *DEC    (5 0)
DCL        &$count    *DEC    (5 0)
DCL        &$offset   *DEC    (5 0)
.
.
.
CHGVAR     &$nbr      %BIN(&$libl 1 2)
CHGVAR     &$count    0
.
.
.
LOOP:
IF         (&$count < &$nbr) THEN(DO)
           CHGVAR    &$count    (&$count +1)
           CHGVAR    &$offset   (&$count * 10 - 7)
           CHGVAR    &$lible    %SST(&$libl &$offset 10))
           .
           .
           .
           GOTO    LOOP
           ENDDO
```

These techniques will work for simple list parameters, which is what you will usually encounter. Mixed lists and "list-within-a-list" parameters contain more complex binary representations within the passed parameter and are beyond the scope of this book.

Debugging a Batch Job

Chapter 33

The STRSRVJOB (Start Service Job) Command

You can use the STRSRVJOB (Start Service Job) command to debug a job from another interactive job. Once you have issued the STRSRVJOB command, you can use any of the debugging commands against the job being debugged.

You can also use STRSRVJOB to debug a batch job submitted to a job queue if you follow this procedure:

1. Use the SBMJOB (Submit Job) command to submit the job to a job queue in a held status:

   ```
   SBMJOB ... HOLD(*YES)
   ```

2. Issue the STRSRVJOB command against the held job. You can determine the qualified name of the job using the WRKJOBQ (Work with Job Queue) command.

3. Issue the STRDBG (Start Debug) command, with the names of all the programs in the job to be debugged. You cannot yet use other debug commands, such as ADDBKP (Add Breakpoint).

4. Release the job, using the RLSJOB (Release Job) command. A display will appear when the job is ready to begin processing.

5. Press F10 to show the command entry display. You can then enter any additional debug commands, such as the ADDBKP (Add Breakpoint) command and the ADDTRC (Add Trace) command.

6. When you press F3 to exit the command entry display, the batch job will start. You can then debug the job, using the normal breakpoint and command entry displays.

7. Use the ENDDBG (End Debug) and ENDSRVJOB (End Service Job) commands when you are finished debugging the batch job.

The LODRUN Command

Chapter 34

Using the LODRUN (Load and Run Media) Command

The LODRUN (Load and Run Media) command allows you to distribute applications for easy installation on another AS/400 system. With the proper preparation by the software vendor or distributor, the user need only load the software media then type the LODRUN command.

LODRUN executes the QINSTAPP program you write.

The LODRUN command requires that you write a CL program that must be called QINSTAPP. The QINSTAPP program must accept the name of the device that contains the software media (usually TAP01). Here is a sample skeleton QINSTAPP program:

```
PGM     PARM(&$device)
DCL     &$device *CHAR 10

/* Restore the application library        */
RSTLIB SAVLIB(application-library)  +
       DEV(&$device)                +
       MBROPT(*ALL)

/* If there is an application initialization */
/* program, or if you want to start the      */
/* application automatically, you can either */
/* CALL or TFRCTL to that program here.      */

RETURN
ENDPGM
```

You would, of course, want to include a message handling procedure within this program. In particular, you will want to check for problems with the &$device parameter. For more information, see *A CL Standard Error-Handling Routine* on page 55.

Follow these steps to create LODRUN media.

Once you have created the QINSTAPP program, you must prepare the distribution media. To prepare a "LODRUN-able" tape or diskette, use the following procedure:

---

1. Initialize the tape or diskette, using the INZTAP (Initialize Tape) or INZDKT (Initialize diskette) command. (For diskettes, specify FMT(*SAVRST).)

2. Clear the QTEMP library: `CLRLIB QTEMP`.

3. Create a copy of the QINSTAPP program in QTEMP using the CRTDUPOBJ (Create Duplicate Object) command.

4. Save the QINSTAPP program to tape or diskette. Use the SAVOBJ (Save Object) command, specifying OBJ(QINSTAPP) LIB(QTEMP), LABEL(*LIB), ENDOPT(*LEAVE), and CLEAR(*ALL).

5. Save any other necessary objects to the tape or diskette, immediately following the QINSTAPP program, using the SAVLIB (Save Library) or SAVOBJ (Save Object) commands. The QINSTAPP program is responsible for restoring these objects.

Note: The LODRUN command will automatically use either TAP01 or T1 as the device name, depending upon the system's device naming conventions. If another device is to be used, the user must specify it (e.g., LODRUN DKT01).

System Values

Chapter 35

Retrieving System Values

System values are specifications that change or control the operation of your system. Use the following CL commands to manipulate, display, or retrieve system values:

CHGSYSVAL (Change System Value)

DSPSYSVAL (Display System Value)

RTVSYSVAL (Retrieve System Value)

WRKSYSVAL (Work with System Values)

Although you cannot pass system values from one program to another, you can retrieve system values, and place them into program variables, using the RTVSYSVAL command.

The chart on the following page lists the valid system values:

System Value Name	Type	Attributes	Shipped Value (USA)	Change Allowed?	Description
QABNORMSW	*SYSCTL	*CHAR 1	0	No	Previous end of system indicator
QACGLVL	*MSG	*CHAR 80	*NONE	Yes[1]	Accounting level
QACTJOB	*ALC	*DEC (5 0)	20	Yes[2]	Initial number of active jobs
QADLACTJ	*ALC	*DEC (5 0)	10	Yes	Additional number of active jobs
QADLSPLA	*ALC	*DEC (5 0)	2048	Yes	Spooling control block additional storage
QADLTOTJ	*ALC	*DEC (5 0)	10	Yes	Additional number of total jobs
QALWUSRDMN [10]	*SEC	*CHAR 500	*ALL	Yes	Lists libraries which will allow user domain objects (*USRSPC, *USRIDX, *USRQ)
QASTLVL	*SYSCTL	*CHAR 10	*BASIC	Yes	User assistance level
QATNPGM	*SYSCTL	*CHAR 20	*ASSIST	Yes[1]	Attention program
QAUDCTL [10]	*SEC	*CHAR 50	*NONE	Yes	Activates/deactivates security auditing
QAUDENDACN [10]	*SEC	*CHAR 10	*NOTIFY	Yes	Action to take when auditing ends
QAUDFRCLVL [10]	*SEC	*DEC (5 0)	*SYS	Yes	Auditing data force level
QAUDLVL	*SEC	*CHAR 160	*NONE	Yes	Security auditing level
QAUTOCFG	*SYSCTL	*CHAR 1	1	Yes	Autoconfigure devices
QAUTOVRT	*SYSCTL	*DEC (5 0)	0	Yes	Autoconfigure virtual devices
QBASACTLVL	*STG	*DEC (5 0)	6	Yes	Base storage pool activity level
QBASPOOL	*STG	*DEC (10 0)	500	Yes	Base storage pool minimum size
QCCSID	*SYSCTL	*DEC (10 0)	65535	Yes[1]	Coded character set identifier
QCHRID	*SYSCTL	*CHAR 20	697 037	Yes[3]	Graphic character set and code page
QCMNRCYLMT	*SYSCTL	*CHAR 20	0 0	Yes[4]	Communications recovery limits
QCNTRYID	*SYSCTL	*CHAR 2	US	Yes[1]	Country identifier
QCONSOLE	*SYSCTL	*CHAR 10	QCONSOLE	No	Console name
QCRTAUT	*SEC	*CHAR 10	*CHANGE	Yes	Create default public authority
QCRTOBJAUD [10]	*SEC	*CHAR 10	*NONE	Yes	Auditing value to use when creating objects
QCTLSBSD	*SYSCTL	*CHAR 20	QSYS/QBASE	Yes[2]	Controlling subsystem
QCURSYM	*EDT	*CHAR 1	$	Yes	Currency symbol
QDATE	*DATTIM	*CHAR 5-6		Yes	System date (*CHAR 5 for Julian date format)
QDATFMT	*EDT	*CHAR 3	MDY	Yes[1]	Date format
QDATSEP	*EDT	*CHAR 1	/	Yes[1]	Date separator
QDAY	*DATTIM	*CHAR 2-3		Yes	Day (*CHAR 3 for Julian date format)
QDBRCVYWT	*SYSCTL	*CHAR 1	0	Yes[2]	Database recovery wait indicator
QDECFMT	*EDT	*CHAR 1	' . '	Yes	Decimal format
QDEVNAMING	*SYSCTL	*CHAR 10	*NORMAL	Yes[5]	Device naming conventions

System Value Name	Type	Attributes	Shipped Value (USA)	Change Allowed?	Description
QDEVRCYACN	*SYSCTL	*CHAR 20	*MSG	Yes[1]	Device I/O error action
QDSCJOBITV	*SYSCTL	*CHAR 10	240	Yes	Time interval before disconnected jobs end
QDSPSGNINF	*SEC	*CHAR 1	0	Yes	Sign-on display information control
QHOUR	*DATTIM	*CHAR 2		Yes	Hour of the day
QHSTLOGSIZ	*MSG	*DEC (5 0)	5000	Yes	Maximum history log records
QIGC	*SYSCTL	*CHAR 1	0	No	DBCS version installed indicator
QIGCCDEFNT	*SYSCTL	*CHAR 20	*NONE	Yes	Double byte code font
QINACTITV	*SEC	*CHAR 10	*NONE	Yes	Inactive job time-out
QINACTMSGQ	*SEC	*CHAR 20	*ENDJOB	Yes	Inactive job message queue
QIPLDATTIM	*SYSCTL	*CHAR 20	*NONE	Yes	Next date and time to automatically IPL
QIPLSTS	*SYSCTL	*CHAR 1	0	No	IPL status indicator
QIPLTYPE	*SYSCTL	*CHAR 1	0	Yes[2]	Type of IPL to perform
QJOBMSGQFL [10]	*ALC	*CHAR 10	*NOWRAP	Yes	Action to take when the job message queue is full
QJOBMSGQMX [10]	*ALC	*DEC (5 0)	16	Yes[1]	Maximum size of job message queue (MB)
QJOBMSGQSZ [9]	*ALC	*DEC (5 0)	16	Yes[1]	Job message queue initial size
QJOBMSGQTL [9]	*ALC	*DEC (5 0)	24	Yes[6]	Job message queue maximum initial size
QJOBSPLA	*ALC	*DEC (5 0)	1536	Yes[7]	Spooling control block initial size
QKBDBUF	*SYSCTL	*CHAR 10	*TYPEAHEAD	Yes[1]	Type ahead and/or attention key option
QKBDTYPE	*SYSCTL	*CHAR 3	USB	Yes	Keyboard language character set
QLANGID	*SYSCTL	*CHAR 3	ENU	Yes[1]	Language identifier
QLEAPADJ	*DATTIM	*CHAR 1	0	Yes	Leap year adjustment
QLMTDEVSSN	*SEC	*CHAR 1	0	Yes	Limit device sessions
QLMTSECOFR	*SEC	*CHAR 1	1	Yes	Limit security officer device access
QMAXACTLVL	*STG	*DEC (5 0)	*NOMAX	Yes	Maximum activity level of system
QMAXSGNACN	*SEC	*CHAR 1	3	Yes	Action to take for failed signon attempts
QMAXSIGN	*SEC	*CHAR 6	15	Yes	Maximum sign-on attempts allowed
QMCHPOOL	*STG	*DEC (10 0)	1500	Yes	Machine storage pool size
QMINUTE	*DATTIM	*CHAR 2		Yes	Minute of the hour
QMODEL	*SYSCTL	*CHAR 4		No	System model number
QMONTH	*DATTIM	*CHAR 2		Yes	Month of the year (not used for Julian date format)
QPFRADJ	*SYSCTL	*CHAR 1	2	Yes[2]	Performance adjustment
QPRBFTR	*MSG	*CHAR 20	*NONE	Yes	Problem log filter
QPRBHLDITV	*MSG	*DEC (5 0)	30	Yes	Problem log hold interval
QPRTDEV	*SYSCTL	*CHAR 10	PRT01	Yes[1]	Printer device description

System Value Name	Type	Attributes	Shipped Value (USA)	Change Allowed?	Description
QPRTKEYFMT	*SYSCTL	*CHAR 10	*PRTHDR	Yes(1)	Print header and/or border information
QPRTTXT	*MSG	*CHAR 30	''	Yes(1)	Print text
QPWDEXPITV	*SEC	*CHAR 6	*NOMAX	Yes(8)	Password expiration interval
QPWDLMTAJC	*SEC	*CHAR 1	0	Yes(8)	Limit adjacent digits in password
QPWDLMTCHR	*SEC	*CHAR 10	*NONE	Yes(8)	Limit characters in password
QPWDLMTREP	*SEC	*CHAR 1	0	Yes(8)	Limit repeating characters in password
QPWDMAXLEN	*SEC	*DEC (5 0)	10	Yes(8)	Maximum password length
QPWDMINLEN	*SEC	*DEC (5 0)	1	Yes(8)	Minimum password length
QPWDPOSDIF	*SEC	*CHAR 1	0	Yes(8)	Limit password character positions
QPWDRQDDGT	*SEC	*CHAR 1	0	Yes(8)	Require digit in password
QPWDRQDDIF	*SEC	*CHAR 1	0	Yes(8)	Duplicate password control
QPWDVLDPGM	*SEC	*CHAR 20	*NONE	Yes(8)	Password validation program
QPWRDWNLMT	*SYSCTL	*DEC (5 0)	600	Yes	Maximum time for PWRDWNSYS *CNTRLD
QPWRRSTIPL	*SYSCTL	*CHAR 1	0	Yes	Automatic IPL after power restored
QRCLSPLSTG	*ALC	*CHAR 10	8	Yes	Reclaim spool storage
QRMTIPL	*SYSCTL	*CHAR 1	0	Yes	Remote power on and IPL
QRMTSIGN	*SEC	*CHAR 20	*FRCSIGNON	Yes	Remote sign-on control
QSCPFCONS	*SYSCTL	*CHAR 1	1	Yes(2)	IPL action with console problem
QSECOND	*DATTIM	*CHAR 2		Yes	Second of the minute
QSECURITY	*SEC	*CHAR 2	10	Yes(2)	System security level
QSFWERRLOG	*MSG	*CHAR 10	*LOG	Yes	Software error logging
QSPCENV	*SYSCTL	*CHAR 10	*NONE	Yes(1)	Special environment
QSRLNBR	*SYSCTL	*CHAR 8		No	System serial number
QSRTSEQ (10)	SYSCTL	*CHAR 20	*HEX	Yes(1)	Sort sequence
QSRVDMP	*MSG	*CHAR 10	*DMPUSRJOB	Yes	Service dump control
QSTRPRTWTR	*SYSCTL	*CHAR 1	1	Yes(2)	Start print writers at IPL
QSTRUPPGM	*SYSCTL	*CHAR 20	QSYS/QSTRUP	Yes(2)	Startup program
QSTSMSG	*MSG	*CHAR 10	*NORMAL	Yes(1)	Display status messages
QSYSLIBL	*LIBL	*CHAR 150	QSYS QSYS2 QHLPSYS QUSRSYS	Yes(1)	System part of the library list
QTIME	*DATTIM	*CHAR 6-9		Yes	Time of day (*CHAR 7-9 for greater precision)
QTIMSEP	*EDT	*CHAR 1	:	Yes(1)	Time separator

System Value Name	Type	Attributes	Shipped Value (USA)	Change Allowed?	Description
QTOTJOB	*ALC	*DEC (5 0)	30	Yes[2]	Initial total number of jobs
QTSEPOOL	*STG	*CHAR 10	*NONE	Yes[1]	Time slice end pool
QUPSDLYTIM	*SYSCTL	*CHAR 20	*CALC	Yes	Uninterruptible power supply delay time
QUPSMSGQ	*SYSCTL	*CHAR 20	QSYS/ QSYSOPR	Yes	Uninterruptible power supply message queue
QUSRLIBL	*LIBL	*CHAR 250	QGPL QTEMP	Yes[1]	User part of the library list
QUTCOFFSET	*DATTIM	*CHAR 5	+0000	Yes	Coordinated universal time offset
QYEAR	*DATTIM	*CHAR 2		Yes	Year

(1) Effective for new jobs started after the change is made.

(2) Effective generally on next IPL.

(3) Effective on next create, change, or override.

(4) Effective the next time a device is varied on.

(5) Effective the next time a device is automatically configured.

(6) Effective the next time a message queue is reinitialized.

(7) Effective on a cold start during installation of a licensed program.

(8) Effective the next time a password is changed.

(9) No longer used with Version 2 Release 3.

(10) New system value with Version 2 Release 3.

Hexadecimal Collating Sequence

Chapter 36

The EBCDIC Character Set

The AS/400 recognizes characters represented by the EBCDIC character set. Many other computer systems, including PCs, use the ASCII character set. The EBCDIC character set consists of 256 characters. The standard ASCII set contains 128 characters, although most systems recognize an extended set of 256 characters.

This chart shows EBCDIC characters and their corresponding ASCII characters; it also lists the decimal, hexadecimal, and binary representations for each character. The characters are shown in hexadecimal collating sequence, which is the standard sequence for both EBCDIC and ASCII. EBCDIC collating sequence sorts uppercase alphabetic characters, then lowercase characters, then numbers; ASCII collating sequence sorts numbers first, then lowercase characters, and finally uppercase characters.

EBCDIC characters below X'40' are control characters and are not usually displayable. ASCII characters below X'20' are control characters.

Decimal	Hexadecimal (English)	Binary	EBCDIC	ASCII
0	00	00000000	NUL	NUL
1	01	00000001	SOH	SOH
2	02	00000010	STX	STX
3	03	00000011	ETX	ETX
4	04	00000100	PF	EOT
5	05	00000101	HT	ENQ
6	06	00000110	LC	ACK
7	07	00000111	DEL	BEL
8	08	00001000	GE	BS
9	09	00001001	RLF	HT
10	0A	00001010	SMM	LF
11	0B	00001011	VT	VT
12	0C	00001100	FF	FF

Decimal	Hexadecimal (English)	Binary	EBCDIC	ASCII
13	0D	00001101	CR	CR
14	0E	00001110	SO	SO
15	0F	00001111	SI	SI
16	10	00010000	DLE	DLE
17	11	00010001	DC1	DC1
18	12	00010010	DC2	DC2
19	13	00010011	TM	DC3
20	14	00010100	ES	DC4
21	15	00010101	NL	NAK
22	16	00010110	BS	SYN
23	17	00010111	IL	ETB
24	18	00011000	CAN	CAN
25	19	00011001	EM	EM
26	1A	00011010	CC	SUB
27	1B	00011011	CU1	ESC
28	1C	00011100	IFS	FS
29	1D	00011101	IGS	GS
30	1E	00011110	IRS	RS
31	1F	00011111	IUS	US
32	20	00100000	DS	(Space)
33	21	00100001	SOS	!
34	22	00100010	FS	"
35	23	00100011		#
36	24	00100100	BYP	$
37	25	00100101	LF	%
38	26	00100110	ETB	&
39	27	00100111	ESC	'
40	28	00101000		(
41	29	00101001		)
42	2A	00101010	SM	*
43	2B	00101011	CU2	+
44	2C	00101100		'
45	2D	00101101	ENQ	-
46	2E	00101110	ACK	.
47	2F	00101111	BEL	/
48	30	00110000		0
49	31	00110001		1
50	32	00110010	SYN	2
51	33	00110011		3
52	34	00110100	PN	4
53	35	00110101	RS	5
54	36	00110110	UC	6

Decimal	Hexadecimal (English)	Binary	EBCDIC	ASCII
55	37	00110111	EOT	7
56	38	00111000		
57	39	00111001		9
58	3A	00111010		:
59	3B	00111011	CU3	;
60	3C	00111100	DC4	<
61	3D	00111101	NAK	=
62	3E	00111110		>
63	3F	00111111	SUB	?
64	40	01000000	(Space)	@
65	41	01000001		A
66	42	01000010		B
67	43	01000011		C
68	44	01000100		D
69	45	01000101		E
70	46	01000110		F
71	47	01000111		G
72	48	01001000		H
73	49	01001001		I
74	4A	01001010	¢	J
75	4B	01001011		K
76	4C	01001100	<	L
77	4D	01001101	(	M
78	4E	01001110	+	N
79	4F	01001111	|	O
80	50	01010000	&	P
81	51	01010001		Q
82	52	01010010		R
83	53	01010011		S
84	54	01010100		T
85	55	01010101		U
86	56	01010110		V
87	57	01010111		W
88	58	01011000		X
89	59	01011001		Y
90	5A	01011010	!	Z
91	5B	01011011	$	[
92	5C	01011100	*	/
93	5D	01011101	)	]
94	5E	01011110	;	^
95	5F	01011111	¬	_
96	60	01100000	-	`

Decimal	Hexadecimal (English)	Binary	EBCDIC	ASCII
97	61	01100001	/	a
98	62	01100010		b
99	63	01100011		c
100	64	01100100		d
101	65	01100101		e
102	66	01100110		f
103	67	01100111		g
104	68	01101000		h
105	69	01101001		i
106	6A	01101010	!	j
107	6B	01101011	,	k
108	6C	01101100	%	l
109	6D	01101101	_	m
110	6E	01101110	>	n
111	6F	01101111	?	o
112	70	01110000		p
113	71	01110001		q
114	72	01110010		r
115	73	01110011		s
116	74	01110100		t
117	75	01110101		u
118	76	01110110		v
119	77	01110111		w
120	78	01111000		x
121	79	01111001		y
122	7A	01111010	:	z
123	7B	01111011	#	{
124	7C	01111100	@	!
125	7D	01111101	'	}
126	7E	01111110	=	~
127	7F	01111111	"	
128	80	10000000		
129	81	10000001	a	
130	82	10000010	b	
131	83	10000011	c	
132	84	10000100	d	
133	85	10000101	e	
134	86	10000110	f	
135	87	10000111	g	
136	88	10001000	h	
137	89	10001001	i	
138	8A	10001010		

Decimal	Hexadecimal (English)	Binary	EBCDIC	ASCII
139	8B	10001011		
140	8C	10001100		
141	8D	10001101		
142	8E	10001110		
143	8F	10001111		
144	90	10010000		
145	91	10010001	j	
146	92	10010010	k	
147	93	10010011	l	
148	94	10010100	m	
149	95	10010101	n	
150	96	10010110	o	
151	97	10010111	p	
152	98	10011100	q	
153	99	10011001	r	
154	9A	10011010		
155	9B	10011011		
156	9C	10011100		
157	9D	10011101		
158	9E	10011110		
159	9F	10011111		
160	A0	10100000		
161	A1	10100001		
162	A2	10100010	s	
163	A3	10100011	t	
164	A4	10100100	u	
165	A5	10100101	v	
166	A6	10100110	w	
167	A7	10100111	x	
168	A8	10101000	y	
169	A9	10101001	z	
170	AA	10101010		
171	AB	10101011		
172	AC	10101100		
173	AD	10101101		
174	AE	10101110		
175	AF	10101111		
176	B0	10110000		
177	B1	10110001		
178	B2	10110010		
179	B3	10110011		
180	B4	10110100		

Decimal	Hexadecimal (English)	Binary	EBCDIC	ASCII
181	B5	10110101		
182	B6	10110110		
183	B7	10110111		
184	B8	10111000		
185	B9	10111001		
186	BA	10111010		
187	BB	10111011		
188	BC	10111100		
189	BD	10111101		
190	BE	10111110		
191	BF	10111111		
192	C0	11000000	{	
193	C1	11000001	A	
194	C2	11000010	B	
195	C3	11000011	C	
196	C4	11000100	D	
197	C5	11000101	E	
198	C6	11000110	F	
199	C7	11000111	G	
200	C8	11001000	H	
201	C9	11001001	I	
202	CA	11001010		
203	CB	11001011		
204	CC	11001100		
205	CD	11001101		
206	CE	11001110		
207	CF	11001111		
208	D0	11010000	}	
209	D1	11010001	J	
210	D2	11010010	K	
211	D3	11010011	L	
212	D4	11010100	M	
213	D5	11010101	N	
214	D6	11010110	O	
215	D7	11010111	P	
216	D8	11011000	Q	
217	D9	11011001	R	
218	DA	11011010		
219	DB	11011011		
220	DC	11011100		
221	DD	11011101		
222	DE	11011110		

Decimal	Hexadecimal (English)	Binary	EBCDIC	ASCII
223	DF	11011111		
224	E0	11100000		
225	E1	11100001		
226	E2	11100010	S	
227	E3	11100011	T	
228	E4	11100100	U	
229	E5	11100101	V	
230	E6	11100110	W	
231	E7	11100111	X	
232	E8	11101000	Y	
233	E9	11101001	Z	
234	EA	11101010		
235	EB	11101011		
236	EC	11101100		
237	ED	11101101		
238	EE	11101110		
239	EF	11101111		
240	F0	11110000	0	
241	F1	11110001	1	
242	F2	11110010	2	
243	F3	11110011	3	
244	F4	1110100	4	
245	F5	11110101	5	
246	F6	11110110	6	
247	F7	11110111	7	
248	F8	11111000	8	
249	F9	11111001	9	
250	FA	11111010		
251	FB	11111011		
252	FC	11111100		
253	FD	11111101		
254	FE	11111110		
255	FF	11111111		

CL Command Summary

This section lists, in alphabetic order, approximately 350 of the most-often-used commands that are shipped with CL. For these commands, a brief description of the command's function is included. Any IBM-supplied file layouts that the command uses are also included, along with those messages for which you can provide a message monitor (MONMSG). Some messages may be monitored by all the CL commands. These MONMSG messages are not listed separately:

MONMSG Messages Available to All Commands
CPF0001 Error found on command.
CPF0010 Command is not supported.
CPF6801 Command prompting ended when user press F3.
CPF9803 Cannot allocate object.
CPF9805 Object destroyed.
CPF9807 One or more libraries in library list deleted.
CPF9808 Cannot allocate one or more library on library list.
CPF9810 Library not found.
CPF9830 Cannot assign library.
CPF9845 Error occurred while opening file.
CPF9846 Error while processing file.
CPF9871 Error occurred while processing.
CPF9901 Request check. Error unmonitored by program.
CPF9999 Function check. Error unmonitored by program.

So that you can easily find related commands, many of the command descriptions are grouped together. For example, the commands that relate to data areas (CHGDTAARA, CRTDTAARA, DLTDTAARA, DSPDTAARA, RTVDTAARA, and WRKDTAARA) are each listed alphabetically, but they are described under the WRKDTAARA entry. Where a command does not list all the MONMSG messages, we've printed an elipses (...) to indicate that there are other messages that may occur in rare instances.

This section does not list individual command parameters. You can easily identify those parameters using CL's command prompting facility.

CL Commands

ADDAUTLE (Add Authorization List Entry) — *See WRKAUTL*
ADDBKP (Add Breakpoint) — *See STRDBG*
ADDBNDDIRE (Add Binding Directory Entry) — *See WRKBNDDIR*
ADDDIRE (Add Directory Entry) — *See WRKDIR*
ADDJOBSCDE (Add Job Schedule Entry) — *See WRKJOBSCDE*
ADDJOBQE (Add Job Queue Entry) — *See WRKSBSD*
ADDLFM (Add Logical File Member) — *See CRTLF*
ADDLIBLE (Add Library List Entry) — *See CHGLIBL*
ADDMSGD (Add Message Description) —*See WRKMSGF*
ADDPFM (Add Physical File Member) — *See CRTPF*
ADDPGM (Add Program) — *See STRDBG*
ADDRPYLE (Add Reply List Entry) — *See WRKRPYLE*
ADDTRC (Add Trace) — *See STRDBG*
ALCOBJ (Allocate Object) — *See WRKOBJLCK*

CALL (Call Program)
> Calls a program, passing control to it. CALL can also pass parameters to the called program.

> **Common MONMSG Messages**
> CPF0006   Errors occurred in command.
> CPF0805   Error found when program started.
> ...

CHGAUTLE (Change Authorization List Entry) — *See WRKAUTL*
CHGCMD (Change Command) — *See WRKCMD*
CHGCMDDFT (Change Command Default) — *See WRKCMD*
CHGCURLIB (Change Current Library) — *See CHGLIBL*
CHGDBG (Change Debug) — *See STRDBG*
CHGDIRE (Change Directory Entry) — *See WRKDIR*
CHGDSPF (Change Display File) — *See CRTDSPF*
CHGDTAARA (Change Data Area) — *See WRKDTAARA*

CHGGRPA (Change Group Attributes) — *See also TFRGRPJOB*
> RTVGRPA (Retrieve Group Attributes)

> These commands manage a job's group attributes. A group job is one of up to 16 interactive jobs that are associated as a group. You can transfer control from one group job to another without ending either of the group jobs. CHGGRPPA changes the group attributes; it can change an interactive job into a group job, or back to a non-group job.

> RTVGRPA copies information about a group job into one or more CL program variables. Use the following parameters to retrieve the information:

CTLCDE	*DEC (3 0)	Control code.
GRPJOB	*CHAR 10	Group job name.
GRPJOBCNT	*DEC (3 0)	Number of jobs in the group.
GRPJOBL	*CHAR 1056	List of up to 16 jobs in the group . Each entry contains the group job name (10), job number

---

		(6), and the group job text (50).
MSGQ	*CHAR 10	Group message queue name.
MSGQLIB	*CHAR 10	MSGQ library name.
PRVGRPJOB	*CHAR 16	Job name (10) and number (6) of the previously active group job.

MONMSG Messages

(All)

CPF1309 Subsystem cannot complete command.
CPF1317 No response from subsystem for job.
CPF1351 Function check occurred.

CHGGRPA:

CPF1305 Changing group job name not allowed.
CPF1306 Specifying GRPJOB(*NONE) not allowed at this time.
CPF1307 Group job already belongs to this group.
CPF1308 Parameters that do not agree were found.
CPF1312 Change group attribute request not valid; job not group job.
CPF1313 Value for parameter not allowed name.
CPF1316 Message queue not allowed as group message queue.
CPF1328 No authority to use queue.
CPF1329 Message queue not found.
CPF1330 Message queue not available.
CPF1331 Message queue not allowed as group message queue.

RTVGRPA:

CPF1311 Job is not a group job.

CHGJOB (Change Job) — *See WRKJOB*
CHGJOBD (Change Job Description) — *See WRKJOBD*
CHGJOBQE (Change Job Queue Entry) — *See WRKSBSD*
CHGJOBSCDE (Change Job Schedule Entry) — *See WRKJOBSCDE*
CHGLF (Change Logical File) — *See CRTLF*
CHGLFM (Change Logical File Member) — *See CRTLF*
CHGLIB (Change Library) —*See WRKLIB*

CHGLIBL (Change Library List)

ADDLIBLE (Add Library List Entry)
CHGCURLIB (Change Current Library)
CHGSYSLIBL (Change System Library List)
DSPLIBL (Display Library List)
EDTLIBL (Edit Library List)
RMVLIBLE (Remove Library List Entry)

These commands manage the current job's library list. The library list indicates which libraries the system searches when locating files, programs, or other AS/400 objects; it also indicates in which order the libraries are searched. CHGLIBL replaces the user portion of the library list with the specified list of libraries. ADDLIBLE and RMVLIBLE add or remove individual entries on the user portion of the library list.

CHGSYSLIBL adds or removes an entry on the system portion of the library list. CHGCURLIB changes the name of the current library. EDTLIBL uses a convenient editing display to add or remove entries in the user portion of the library list. DSPLIBL displays the entire library list. The system will search the libraries in the library list in the following order:

(1) System portion

(2) Product library

(3) Current library

(4) User portion

Files Used

DSPLIBL:

QSYS/QPRTLIBL   *PRTF   Library list printer file.

Common MONMSG Messages

(All except DSPLIBL and EDTLIBL)
CPF2106   Library list not changed.
CPF2110   Library not found.
CPF2113   Cannot allocate library.
CPF2182   Not authorized to library.

ADDLIBLE:
CPF2103   Library already exists in library list.
CPF2118   Library not added.
...

CHGCURLIB:
...

CHGLIBL:
CPF2184   Library list not replaced.

CHGSYSLIBL:
CPF2103   Library already exists in library list.
CPF2118   Library not added.
CPF2128   Library not in system portion of library list.
...

DSPLIBL:
CPF2113   Cannot allocate library.
CPF2179   Cannot display library.
CPF2182   Not authorized to library.
CPF9847   Error occurred while closing file.
...

EDTLIBL:
CPF2106   Library list not changed.
CPF2184   Library list not replaced.

RMVLIBLE:
CPF2103   Library already exists in library list.
CPF2104   Library not removed from the library list.
CPF2118   Library not added.
...

CHGMNU (Change Menu) — *See WRKMNU*
CHGMOD (Change Module) — *See WRKMOD*

CHGMSGD (Change Message Description) — *See WRKMSGF*

CHGMSGQ (Change Message Queue) — *See WRKMSGQ*

CHGNETA (Change Network Attributes)

DSPNETA (Display Network Attributes)

RTVNETA (Retrieve Network Attributes)

These commands manage the system's network attributes, such as the system name and the local network ID. CHGNETA changes the network attributes; DSPNETA displays network attributes.

RTVNETA copies one or more network attributes into a variable in the CL program. The following parameters are used to retrieve the most often used information:

DFTMODE	*CHAR 8	Default APPC/APPN mode.
LCLCPNAME	*CHAR 8	Local control point name.
LCLLOCNAME	*CHAR 8	Local location name.
LCLNETID	*CHAR 8	Local network identifier.
MSGQ	*CHAR 10	SNADS message queue for unassigned users.
MSGQLIB	*CHAR 10	MSGQ library.
NODETYPE	*CHAR 8	APPN node type.
OUTQ	*CHAR 10	SNADS output queue for unassigned users.
OUTQLIB	*CHAR 10	OUTQ library.
PCSACC	*CHAR 10	PC Support request access value.
PCSACCLIB	*CHAR 10	Library name for PCSACC program.
PNDSYSNAME	*CHAR 8	Pending system name.
SYSNAME	*CHAR 8	System name.

...

Files Used

DSPNETA:

QSYS/QANFDNTF	*PF	Model OUTFILE for network attributes.
QSYS/QPDSPNET	*PRTF	Network attributes printer file.

Common MONMSG Messages

CHGNETA:

CPF1007 Character is not valid.
CPF1066 Network attributes not changed.
CPF1097 No authority to change certain network attributes.
CPF1844 Cannot access network attribute.
CPF9801 Object not found.
CPF9899 Error occurred during processing of command.

...

DSPNETA:

CPF9847 Error occurred while closing file.
CPF9850 Override of printer file not allowed.
CPF9851 Overflow value too small.

RTVNETA:

CPF1844 Cannot access network attribute.

CHGOBJD (Change Object Description) — *See WRKOBJ*

CHGOBJOWN (Change Object Owner) — *See WRKOBJOWN*
CHGOUTQ (Change Output Queue) — *See WRKOUTQ*
CHGPF (Change Physical File) — *See CRTPF*
CHGPFM (Change Physical File Member) — *See CRTPF*
CHGPGM (Change Program) — *See WRKPGM*
CHGPGMVAR (Change Program Variable) — *See STRDBG*
CHGPRF (Change Profile) — *See WRKUSRPRF*
CHGPRTF (Change Printer File) — *See CRTPRTF*

CHGPWD (Change Password) — *See also WRKUSRPRF*
CHKPWD (Check Password)
These commands work with the current user's password. CHGPWD allows the user to change his/her password. CHKPWD verifies the password of the user who signed on.

MONMSG Messages

CHGPWD:

CPF22C0	Password does not meet password rules.
CPF22C2	Password too short.
CPF22C3	Password too long.
CPF22C4	Password matches one of 32 previous passwords.
CPF22C5	Password contains invalid character.
CPF22C6	Password contains two numbers next to each other.
CPF22C7	Password contains a character used more than once.
CPF22C8	Same character in same position as previous password.
CPF22C9	Password must contain a number.
CPF22D1	Password cannot be same as user ID.
CPF22D2	Password approval program not found.
CPF22D3	Password approval program signaled an error.
CPF22D4	Not allowed to use password approval program.
CPF22D5	Parameters in password approval program not correct.
CPF2356	Password not changed.

CHKPWD:

CPF2362	Password not correct.
CPF2363	Only 1 attempt left to check password.
CPF2364	Maximum number of attempts to check password reached.

CHGRPYLE (Change Reply List Entry) — *See WRKRPYLE*
CHGSAVF (Change Save File) —*See CRTSAVF*
CHGSBSD (Change Subsystem Description) — *See WRKSBS*
CHGSPLFA (Change Spooled File Attributes) — *See WRKSPLF*
CHGSRCPF (Change Source Physical File) — *See CRTSRCPF*
CHGSRVPGM (Change Service Program) — *See WRKSRVPGM*
CHGSYSLIBL (Change System Library List) — *See CHGLIBL*
CHGSYSVAL (Change System Value) — *See WRKSYSVAL*
CHGUSRPRF (Change User Profile) — *See WRKUSRPRF*

CHGVAR (Change Variable)
Changes the value of all or part of a CL program variable, to the value of a constant, another variable, the evaluation of an expression, or the evaluation of a built-in function, such as %SST or %BIN.

MONMSG Messages
CPF0816   %SWITCH mask not valid.

CHGWTR (Change Writer) — *See WRKWTR*

CHKDKT (Check Diskette)

Searches a diskette for a specific volume label, file, and/or creation date. CHKDKT returns an error message if the search fails.

MONMSG Messages

CPF6112	Diskette has extended label area that is not searched.
CPF6162	Diskette does not contain specified identifiers.
CPF6164	Cannot read diskette.
CPF6165	Device is not ready.
CPF6708	Command ended due to error.
CPF6716	Device not a diskette device.
CPF6718	Cannot allocate device.
CPF9814	Device not found.
CPF9825	Not authorized to device.

CHKOBJ (Check Object) — *See also CPROBJ, CRTDUPOBJ, DMPOBJ, MOVOBJ, RNMOBJ, SAVOBJ, WRKOBJ, WRKOBJLCK*

Checks for the existence of an object, and optionally checks for the user's authority to an object. CHKOBJ returns an error message if either the existence or the authority check fails.

MONMSG Messages

CPF9801	Object not found.
CPF9802	Not authorized to object.
CPF9815	Member not found.
CPF9820	Not authorized to use library.
CPF9899	Error occurred during processing of command.

CHKPWD (Check Password) — *See CHGPWD*

CHKRCDLCK (Check Record Locks) — *See WRKOBJLCK*

CHKTAP (Check Tape)

CLOF (Close File) — *See OPNDBF*

CLRJOBQ (Clear Job Queue) — *See WRKJOBQ*

CLRLIB (Clear Library) — *See WRKLIB*

CLRMSGQ (Clear Message Queue) — *See WRKMSGQ*

CLROUTQ (Clear Output Queue) — *See WRKOUTQ*

CLRPFM (Clear Physical File Member) — *See CRTPF*

CLRSAVF (Clear Save File) — *See CRTSAVF*

CLRTRCDTA (Clear Trace Data) — *See STRDBG*

CPROBJ (Compress Object) — *See also CHKOBJ, CRTDUPOBJ, DMPOBJ, MOVOBJ, RNMOBJ, SAVOBJ, WRKOBJ, WRKOBJLCK*

DCPOBJ (Decompress Object)

These commands manage object compression. Compression reduces the amount of disk storage required to store an object; CPROBJ compresses programs, panel groups, menus, display files, and printer files. DCPOBJ returns them to their original form for processing. If you use a compressed object, the system will automatically decompress it first.

Common MONMSG Messages

(All)

CPF2110	Library not found.
CPF2113	Cannot allocate library.
CPF3B01	Cannot compress or decompress object.
CPF3B02	Cannot compress or decompress file.
CPF3B08	Cannot allocate object.

CPF9802 Not authorized to object.
CPF9806 Cannot perform function for object.
CPF9811 Program not found.
CPF9812 File not found.
CPF9821 Not authorized to program.
CPF9822 Not authorized to file.
CPF9838 User profile storage limit exceeded.
...

CPROBJ:
CPF3B03 No objects compressed.
CPF3B04 nn objects compressed; nn not compressed; nn not
         included.
CPF3B09 Not all subsystems ended.
CPF3B10 Cannot compress program.

DCPOBJ:
CPF3B05 No objects decompressed.
CPF3B06 nn objects decompressed; nn not decompressed; nn
         not included.

CPYF (Copy File)

Copies all or part of a file. CPYF can copy from one database file to
another, or between files and external devices, such as tapes.

Files Used
QSYS/QSYSPRT   *PRTF   Copy file printer file.

Common MONMSG Messages
CPF2816 File not copied because of error.
CPF2817 Copy command ended because of error.
CPF2858 File attributes not valid for printed output.
CPF2859 Shared open data path not allowed.
CPF2864 Not authorized to file.
CPF2875 Wrong file member or label opened.
CPF2883 Error creating file.
CPF2888 Member not added to file because of error.
CPF2909 Error clearing member.
CPF2949 Error closing member.
CPF2952 Error opening file.
CPF2968 Position error occurred copying file.
CPF2971 Error reading member.
CPF2972 Error writing to member.
CPF2975 Error while reading from keyed file.
CPF2976 Number of errors greater than ERRLVL value.
CPF3140 Initialize or copy of member canceled.
CPF3143 Increments not allowed for member.
CPF3148 New records need too much space for member.
CPF3150 Data base copy failed for member.
...

CPYFRMDKT (Copy from Diskette) — *See also CPYF*
CPYTODKT (Copy to Diskette)

These commands copy one or more data files between a diskette and the
system. CPYFRMDKT copies from a diskette; CPYTODKT copies files
to a diskette.

Files Used

CPYFRMDKT:

QSYS/QSYSPRT   *PRTF   Copy file printer file.

Common MONMSG Messages

(All)

CPF2816	File not copied because of error.
CPF2817	Copy command ended because of error.
CPF2859	Shared open data path not allowed.
CPF2875	Wrong file member or label opened.
CPF2949	Error closing member.
CPF2952	Error opening file.
CPF2971	Error reading member.
CPF2972	Error writing to member.

...

CPYFRMDKT:

CPF2858	File attributes not valid for printed output.
CPF2888	Member not added to file because of error.
CPF2909	Error clearing member.

...

CPYTODKT:

CPF2864	Not authorized to file.
CPF2968	Position error occurred copying file.

CPYFRMQRYF (Copy From Query File) — *See also OPNQRYF*

Copies all or part of a file opened by the OPNQRYF command to a database file, a diskette file, a tape file, or to the printer.

Files Used

QSYS/QSYSPRT   *PRTF   Copy file printer file.

Common MONMSG Messages

CPF2816	File not copied because of error.
CPF2817	Copy command ended because of error.
CPF2858	File attributes not valid for printed output.
CPF2859	Shared open data path not allowed.
CPF2864	Not authorized to file.
CPF2875	Wrong file member or label opened.
CPF2883	Error creating file.
CPF2888	Member not added to file because of error.
CPF2909	Error clearing member.
CPF2949	Error closing member.
CPF2952	Error opening file.
CPF2971	Error reading member.
CPF2972	Error writing to member.
CPF2975	Error while reading from keyed file.
CPF2976	Number of errors greater than ERRLVL value.
CPF3140	Initialize or copy of member canceled.
CPF3143	Increments not allowed for member.
CPF3148	New records need too much space for member.
CPF3150	Data base copy failed for member.

...

CPYFRMTAP (Copy from Tape)

CPYTOTAP (Copy to Tape)

These commands copy one or more data files between a tape and the system. CPYFRMTAP copies from a tape; CPYTOTAP copies files to a tape.

Files Used

QSYS/QSYSPRT	*PRTF	Copy file printer file.

Common MONMSG Messages

(All)

CPF2816	File not copied because of error.
CPF2817	Copy command ended because of error.
CPF2859	Shared open data path not allowed.
CPF2875	Wrong file member or label opened.
CPF2949	Error closing member.
CPF2952	Error opening file.
CPF2971	Error reading member.
CPF2972	Error writing to member.

...

CPYFRMTAP:

CPF2858	File attributes not valid for printed output.
CPF2888	Member not added to file because of error.
CPF2909	Error clearing member.

...

CPYTOTAP:

CPF2864	Not authorized to file.
CPF2968	Position error occurred copying file.

...

CPYLIB (Copy Library) — *See WRKLIB*
CPYSPLF (Copy Spooled File) — *See WRKSPLF*
CPYSRCF (Copy Source File) — *See CRTSRCPF*
CPYTODKT (Copy to Diskette) — *See CPYFRMDKT*
CPYTOTAP (Copy to Tape) — *See CPTFRMTAP*
CRTAUTL (Create Authorization List) — *See WRKAUTL*
CRTBNDDIR (Create Binding Directory) — *See WRKBNDDIR*

CRTCLPGM (Create Control Language Program) — *See also DLTPGM*

Creates an executable CL program object from a CL source member.

Files Used

QGPL/QCLSRC	*PF	Source default input file.
QSYS/QSYSPRT	*PRTF	Source listing printer file.

Common MONMSG Messages

CPF0801	Program not created.
CPF0807	File containing compiler printout not opened.
CPF0808	Error in compiler-created code.
CPF0815	CL program cannot be created for previous release.
CPF3202	File in use.
CPF3203	Cannot allocate object for file.
CPF3224	Not authorized to perform operation on file.

...

CRTCMD (Create Command) — *See WRKCMD*

CRTDSPF (Create Display File) — *See also DLTF, OVRDSPF*

CHGDSPF (Change Display File)

These commands manage display device files. A display file describes one or more display screens to the system. Display files contain no data. CRTDSPF creates a display file, usually using the Data Description Specifications (DDS) stored in a source file member. CHGDSPF changes some of the properties of the display file.

Files Used

CRTDSPF:

QGPL/QDDSSRC	*PF	Source default input file.
QSYS/QPDDSSRC	*PRTF	Source listing printer file.

MONMSG Messages

CHGDSPF:

CPF7304   File not changed.
CPF7308   nn files not changed. n files changed.

CRTDSPF:

CPF7302   File not created.

CRTDTAARA (Create Data Area) — *See WRKDTAARA*

CRTDTAQ (Create Data Queue) — *See WRKDTAQ*

CRTDUPOBJ (Create Duplicate Object) — *See also CHKOBJ, CPROBJ, DMPOBJ, MOVOBJ, RNMOBJ, SAVOBJ, WRKOBJ, WRKOBJLCK*

Duplicates a single object or a group of objects.

Common MONMSG Messages

CPF2105   Object not found.
CPF2109   NEWOBJ must be *SAME when OBJ parameter is *ALL or generic name.
CPF2110   Library not found.
CPF2113   Cannot allocate library.
CPF2116   DATA(*YES) specified and *ALL or *FILE not in OBJTYPE list.
CPF2122   Storage limit exceeded for user profile.
CPF2123   No objects of specified name or type exist in library.
CPF2130   nn objects duplicated. nn objects not duplicated.
CPF2151   Operation failed.
CPF2152   This type of object cannot be created into QTEMP.
CPF2162   Duplication of all objects in library not allowed.
CPF2182   Not authorized to library.
CPF2185   TOLIB or NEWOBJ parameters not correct
CPF2186   Object cannot be created.
CPF9827   Object cannot be created.
...

CRTJOBD (Create Job Description) — *See WRKJOBD*

CRTJOBQ (Create Job Queue) — *See WRKJOBQ*

CRTLF (Create Logical File) — *See also DLTF, OVRDBF, RMVM, RNMM*

ADDLFM (Add Logical File Member)
CHGLF (Change Logical File)
CHGLFM (Change Logical File Member)

These commands manage logical files. Logical files describe different views of the information in physical database files, perhaps presenting the data in different order, to show only some of the fields in the file, or to select only certain records from the file. Logical files themselves contain no data. CRTLF creates a new logical file, using the data description specifications (DDS) stored in a source file member. CHGLF changes certain attributes of an existing logical file.

ADDLFM adds a file member to a logical file, while CHGLFM changes certain properties of a logical file member. A member is an individual grouping of records in the database file.

Files Used

CRTLF:

QGPL/QDDSSRC	*PF	Source default input file.
QSYS/QPDDSSRC	*PRTF	Source listing printer file.

Common MONMSG Messages

ADDLFM:

CPF3204	Cannot find object needed for file.
CPF7306	Member not added to file.

CHGLF:

CPF326A	Operation not successful for file.
CPF7304	File not changed.

CHGLFM:

CPF3288	Member not changed.

CRTLF:

CPF3204	Cannot find object needed for file.
CPF323C	QRECOVERY library could not be allocated.
CPF7302	File not created.

...

CRTLIB (Create Library) — *See WRKLIB*
CRTMNU (Create Menu) — *See WRKMNU*
CRTMSGF (Create Message File) — *See WRKMSGF*
CRTMSGQ (Create Message Queue) — *See WRKMSGQ*
CRTOUTQ (Create Output Queue) — *See WRKOUTQ*
CRTPF (Create Physical File) — *See also CRTSRCPF, DLTF, OVRDBF, RMVM, RNMM*
ADDPFM (Add Physical File Member)
CHGPF (Change Physical File)
CHGPFM (Change Physical File Member)
CLRPFM (Clear Physical File Member)
DSPPFM (Display Physical File Member)
INZPFM (Initialize Physical File Member)
RGZPFM (Reorganize Physical File Member)

These commands manage physical files. Physical files contain data. CRTPF creates a new physical file, usually using the data description specifications (DDS) stored in a source file member. You can also create a physical file without DDS, specifying only the record length. CHGPF changes certain attributes of an existing physical file.

ADDPFM adds a file member to a physical file, while CHGPFM changes certain properties of a physical file member. A member is an individual grouping of records in the database file. CLRPFM removes all the data from a file member without deleting the file. DSPPFM displays the data records in a file member. INZPFM initializes a file member, creating default records or deleted records, for files that are processed in arrival sequence or by relative record numbers. RGZPFM removes deleted records from a file member, thus compressing it, and optionally reorganizes that member.

Files Used

CRTPF:

QGPL/QDDSSRC	*PF	Source default input file.
QSYS/QPDDSSRC	*PRTF	Source listing printer file.

Common MONMSG Messages

ADDPFM:

CPF3204	Cannot find object needed for file.
CPF7306	Member not added to file.

CHGPF:

CPF326A	Operation not successful for file.
CPF7304	File not changed.

CHGPFM:

CPF3288	Member not changed.

CLRPFM:

CPF3130	Member already in use.
CPF3133	File contains no members.
CPF3136	File not allowed on command.
CPF3137	No authority to clear, initialize, or copy member.
CPF3141	Member not found.
CPF3142	File not found.
CPF3144	Member not cleared or initialized.
CPF3156	File in use.
CPF3203	Cannot allocate object for file.
...	

CRTPF:

CPF3204	Cannot find object needed for file.
CPF7302	File not created.
...	

DSPPFM:

CPF8056	File not a physical file.
CPF9812	File not found.
CPF9820	Not authorized to use library.
CPF9822	Not authorized to file.
CPF9847	Error occurred while closing file.

INZPFM:

CPF3130	Member already in use.
CPF3131	Cannot initialize member with default records.
CPF3133	File contains no members.
CPF3136	File not allowed on command.
CPF3137	No authority to clear, initialize, or copy member.
CPF3140	Initialize or copy of member canceled.
CPF3141	Member not found.
CPF3142	File not found.
CPF3144	Member not cleared or initialized.
CPF3148	New records need too much space for member.
CPF3156	File in use.
CPF3180	Member not initialized.
CPF320B	Operation was not valid for database file.

CPF9801 Object not found.
CPF9820 Not authorized to use library.
...

RGZPFM:
CPF2981 Member not reorganized.
CPF3135 Access path for member already in use.
CPF9801 Object not found.
CPF9809 Library cannot be accessed.
CPF9820 Not authorized to use library.
...

CRTPGM (Create Program) — *See WRKPGM*
CRTPNLGRP (Create Panel Group) — *See WRKPNLGRP*
CRTPRTF (Create Printer File) — *See also DLTF, OVRPRTF*
CHGPRTF (Change Printer File)
These commands manage printer device files, which define a report to be printed. CRTPRTF creates a printer file using Data Description Specifications (DDS) stored in a source physical file. CHGPRTF changes certain attributes of a printer file.

Files Used
CRTPRTF:

QGPL/QDDSSRC	*PF	Source default input file.
QSYS/QPDDSSRC	*PRTF	Source listing printer file.

MONMSG Messages
CHGPRTF:
CPF7304 File not changed.
CPF7308 nn files not changed. nn files changed.

CRTPRTF:
CPF7302 File not created.

CRTSAVF (Create Save File) — *See also OVRSAVF, SAVSAVFDTA*
CHGSAVF (Change Save File)
CLRSAVF (Clear Save File)
DSPSAVF (Display Save File)
These commands manage online save files, which the save/restore commands use to hold data instead of copying it to magnetic media (tape or diskette). CRTSAVF creates an online save file. CLRSAVF clears all the data from an online save file. DSPSAVF displays a description of each item saved in the save file; it does not display the actual save file data.

Files Used
DSPSAVF:

QSYS/QPSRODSP	*PRTF	Save file save/restore information printer file.

MONMSG Messages
(All except CHGSAVF, CRTSAVF)
CPF3782 File not a save file.
CPF3812 Save file in use.
CPF9812 File not found.
CPF9820 Not authorized to use library.
CPF9822 Not authorized to file.

CHGSAVF:
CPF7304 File not changed.

CRTSAVF:

CPF7302 File not created.

DSPSAVF:

CPF3704 Request ended; data management error occurred.
CPF3743 File cannot be restored, displayed, or listed.
CPF3793 Machine storage limit reached.
CPF9806 Cannot perform function for object.
CPF9809 Library cannot be accessed.
CPF9850 Override of printer file not allowed.
CPF9851 Overflow value for file too small.

CRTSBSD (Create Subsystem Description) — See WRKSBS

CRTSRCPF (Create Source Physical File) — See also CRTPF, DLTF

CHGSRCPF (Change Source Physical File)
CPYSRCF (Copy Source File)

These commands manage source physical files. A source physical file is a special type of database file that stores source records used with the IBM-supplied compilers, such as the RPG compiler or the DDS processor. The AS/400 predefines source file records with three fields, SRCSEQ (Sequence number), SRCDAT (Date last changed), and SRCDTA (Source data). CRTSRCPF creates a new source physical file, while CHGSRCPF changes certain properties of a source file. CPYSRCF copies one or more members of a source file to another source file, or prints the contents of a source file member.

Files Used

CPYSRCPF:

QSYS/QSYSPRT   *PRTF   Copy file printer file.

Common MONMSG Messages

CHGSRCPF:

CPF326A Operation not successful for file.
CPF7304 File not changed.

CPYSRCF:

CPF2816 File not copied because of error.
CPF2817 Copy command ended because of error.
CPF2858 File attributes not valid for printed output.
CPF2859 Shared open data path not allowed.
CPF2864 Not authorized to file.
CPF2875 Wrong file member or label opened.
CPF2888 Member not added to file because of error.
CPF2909 Error clearing member.
CPF2949 Error closing member.
CPF2952 Error opening file.
CPF2968 Position error occurred copying file.
CPF2971 Error reading member.
CPF2972 Error writing to member.
CPF3140 Initialize or copy of member canceled.
CPF3143 Increments not allowed for member.
CPF3148 New records need too much space for member.
CPF3150 Data base copy failed for member.
...

CRTSRCPF:

CPF7302 File not created.
...

CRTSRVPGM (Create Service Program) — *See WRKSRVPGM*

CRTUSRPRF (Create User Profile) — *See WRKUSRPRF*

CVTDAT (Convert Date)

Converts the format of a valid date value in a CL program from one format to another

<u>MONMSG Messages</u>

CPF0550   Date too short for specified format.
CPF0551   Separators in date are not valid.
CPF0552   Date contains misplaced or extra separators.
CPF0553   Date contains too many or too few numeric characters.
CPF0554   Variable specified too short for converted date format.
CPF0555   Date not in specified format or date not valid.
CPF0556   Date contains two or more kinds of separators.
CPF0557   Date outside allowed range.

DCL (Declare CL Variable) — *See also DCLF*

Defines program variables used in CL programs, naming the variable, and describing its attributes.

<u>MONMSG Messages</u>
(None)

DCLF (Declare File) — *See also DCL*

Defines a file to be used by a CL program. You can declare only one file, either a display file or a database file, in a CL program. DCLF makes the file available to the program and implictly declares each field in the file as a CL program variable.

<u>MONMSG Messages</u>
(None)

DCPOBJ (Decompress Object) — *See CPROBJ*

DLCOBJ (Deallocate Object) — *See WRKOBJLCK*

DLTAUTL (Delete Authorization List) — *See WRKAUTL*

DLTBNDDIR (Delete Binding Directory) — *See WRKBNDDIR*

DLTCMD (Delete Command) — *See WRKCMD*

DLTDTAARA (Delete Data Area) — *See WRKDTAARA*

DLTDTAQ (Delete Data Queue) — *See WRKDTAQ*

DLTF (Delete File) — *See also CRTDSPF, CRTLF, CRTPF, CRTPRTF, CRTSRCPF*

Deletes one or more files from the system, freeing the storage occupied by the file(s). DLTF removes any file, regardless of its type (physical file, logical file, display file, etc.).

<u>Common MONMSG Messages</u>

CPF0601   Not allowed to do operation to file.
CPF0605   Device file saved with storage freed.
CPF0607   File deleted by another job.
CPF0610   File not available.
CPF0675   Device file is in use.
CPF2105   Object not found.
CPF2110   Library not found.
CPF2114   Cannot allocate object.
CPF2117   nn objects deleted. nn objects not deleted.
CPF2182   Not authorized to library.
CPF2189   Not authorized to object.

CPF2190   Not able to do remote delete or rename request.
CPF3203   Cannot allocate object for file.
CPF3220   Cannot do operation on file.
CPF326A   Operation not successful for file.
CPF3273   File or member not created, deleted or changed.
...

DLTJOBD (Delete Job Description) — *See WRKJOBD*
DLTJOBQ (Delete Job Queue) — *See WRKJOBQ*
DLTLIB (Delete Library) — *See WRKLIB*
DLTMNU (Delete Menu) — *See WRKMNU*
DLTMOD (Delete Module) — *See WRKMOD*
DLTMSGF (Delete Message File) — *See WRKMSGF*
DLTMSGQ (Delete Message Queue) — *See WRKMSGQ*
DLTOUTQ (Delete Output Queue) — *See WRKOUTQ*

DLTOVR (Delete Override) — *See also DSPOVR, OVRDBF, OVRDSPF, OVRMSGF, OVRPRTF, OVRSAVF*

Deletes one or more overrides that are in effect at a single program invocation level.

MONMSG Messages
CPF9841   Override not found at current call level.

DLTPGM (Delete Program) — *See WRKPGM*
DLTPNLGRP (Delete Panel Group) — *See WRKPNLGRP*
DLTSBSD (Delete Subsystem Description) — *See WRKSBS*
DLTSPLF (Delete Spooled File) — *See WRKSPLF*
DLTSRVPGM (Delete Service Program) — *See WRKSRVPGM*
DLTUSRPRF (Delete User Profile) — *See WRKUSRPRF*

DLYJOB (Delay Job)

Causes a CL program to pause for a specified number of seconds, or until a specified time of day.

MONMSG Messages
(None)

DMPCLPGM (Dump CL Program)

Prints a report, showing the values of all variables in a CL program and all messages on the program's message queue. After spooling the report, the program resumes. This report is useful for problem analysis.

Files Used
QSYS/QPPGMDMP   *PRTF   Program dump printer file.

MONMSG Messages
CPF0570   Unable to dump CL program.

DMPJOB (Dump Job) — *See WRKJOB*
DMPOBJ (Dump Object) — *See also CHKOBJ, CPROBJ, CRTDUPOBJ, MOVOBJ, RNMOBJ, SAVOBJ, WRKOBJ, WRKOBJLCK*

Prints a report showing the contents and/or properties of an object. This report is useful for problem analysis.

Files used
QSYS/QPSRVDMP   *PRTF   Service dump printer file.

Common MONMSG Messages
CPF3562   Object not found.
CPF3673   Not authorized to library.
CPF3925   Cannot open file.

CPF3947 Library not available.
CPF3948 Library previously deleted.
CPF3950 Error message received for file. Request ended.
CPF3951 File cannot be overridden by file name.
CPF3969 Error during close of file. Output may not be
         complete.
...

DO (Do)
ENDDO (End Do)
DO and ENDDO mark the start and end of a group of commands that
will be processed as a group. DO is usually used in conjunction with the
IF or ELSE commands to allow conditional processing in a CL program.
Every DO command in a CL program must be paired with a matching
ENDDO command.

MONMSG Messages
(None)

DSCJOB (Disconnect Job) — See also SIGNOFF
Disconnects the interactive job(s) at a workstation, and displays a sign on
display. The disconnected jobs are not ended, and the user can resume
work by signing on.

MONMSG Messages
CPF1317 No response from subsystem for job.
CPF1321 Job not found.
CPF1332 End of duplicate job names.
CPF1333 DSCJOB command not allowed for this job now.
CPF1344 Not authorized to control job.
CPF1351 Function check occurred in subsystem for job.
CPF1353 DSCJOB command not allowed for this job now.
CPF1354 DSCJOB command not allowed for this job now.
CPF1355 DSCJOB command not allowed for this job.
CPF1358 DSCJOB not allowed for Server jobs.
CPF1385 DSCJOB command not allowed for this job now.
CPF1386 DSCJOB is not valid.
CPF1387 DSCJOB is not valid.
CPF1388 DSCJOB command not allowed at this device.
CPF1389 DSCJOB command not allowed for this job now.
CPF1391 DSCJOB command not allowed for this job now.
CPF1656 Disconnect job not allowed for test request jobs.

DSPAUTL (Display Authorization List) — See WRKAUTL
DSPAUTLOBJ (Display Authorization List Objects) — See
     WRKAUTL

DSPAUTUSR (Display Authorized Users)
Displays or prints an alphabetic list of the authorized users on a system.

Files Used
QSYS/QPAUTUSR   *PRTF Authorized users printer
                              file.

MONMSG Messages
CPF2225 Not able to allocate internal system object.
CPF2237 Not authorized to display list of users.

DSPBKP (Display Breakpoints) — See STRDBG
DSPBNDDIR (Display Binding Directory) — See WRKBNDDIR

DSPCMD (Display Command) — *See WRKCMD*

DSPDBG (Display Debug) — *See STRDBG*

DSPDBR (Display Database Relations)

Shows relational information about a database file, i.e., files (or members) that are dependent upon a file.

Files Used

QSYS/QADSPDBR	*PF	Model OUTFILE.
QSYS/QPDSPDBR	*PRTF	Database file relationships printer file.

MONMSG Messages

CPF3010	No database files found.
CPF3012	File not found.
CPF3014	No file specified can be displayed.
CPF3028	Record format not found.
CPF3029	Member not found.
CPF3052	Description for file not available.
CPF3061	Record format not found.
CPF3063	Output file not physical file.
CPF3064	Library not found.
CPF3066	Error creating output file.
CPF3067	Error while opening file.
CPF3068	Error while writing to file.
CPF3069	Error while closing file.
CPF3070	Error creating member.
CPF3072	File is a system file.
CPF3074	Not authorized to library.
CPF3075	Library not available.
CPF3076	Error occurred when on display.
CPF3077	Error occurred when canceling display.
CPF3084	Error clearing member.

DSPDIR (Display Directory) — *See WRKDIR*

DSPDKT (Display Diskette)

Shows information about a diskette. In addition to volume and data file label information, DSPDKT can show information about objects that have been saved on the diskette.

Files Used

QSYS/QPDSPDKT	*PRTF	Printer file for basic exchange format.
QSYS/QPSRODSP	*PRTF	Printer file for save/restore format.

Common MONMSG Messages

CPF3743	File cannot be restored, displayed, or listed.
CPF3791	End of file.
CPF3793	Machine storage limit reached.
CPF3796	Storage limit exceeded for user profile.
CPF6017	Display diskette ended; previous error occurred.
CPF6716	Device not a diskette device.
CPF6718	Cannot allocate device.
CPF9814	Device not found.
CPF9825	Not authorized to device.
CPF9851	Overflow value for file too small.

...

DSPDTAARA (Display Data Area) — *See WRKDTAARA*

DSPFD (Display File Description)

Shows information about a file. Different information is shown for different types of files, and you can specify different types of information for some file types.

Files Used

QSYS/QAFDACCP	*PF	Model OUTFILE for access path information.
QSYS/QAFDBASI	*PF	Model OUTFILE for basic file information.
QSYS/QAFDBSC	*PF	Model OUTFILE for BSC file information.
QSYS/QAFDCMN	*PF	Model OUTFILE for communications file information.
QSYS/QAFDDDM	*PF	Model OUTFILE for DDM file information.
QSYS/QAFDDKT	*PF	Model OUTFILE for diskette file information.
QSYS/QAFDDSP	*PF	Model OUTFILE for display file information.
QSYS/QAFDICF	*PF	Model OUTFILE for ICF files information.
QSYS/QAFDJOIN	*PF	Model OUTFILE for join logical file information.
QSYS/QAFDLGL	*PF	Model OUTFILE for logical file information.
QSYS/QAFDMBR	*PF	Model OUTFILE for database file member information.
QSYS/QAFDMBRL	*PF	Model OUTFILE for database member list.
QSYS/QAFDPHY	*PF	Model OUTFILE for physical file information.
QSYS/QAFDPRT	*PF	Model OUTFILE for printer file information.
QSYS/QAFDRFMT	*PF	Model OUTFILE for record format information.
QSYS/QAFDSAV	*PF	Model OUTFILE for save file information.
QSYS/QAFDSELO	*PF	Model OUTFILE for select/omit information.
QSYS/QAFDSPOL	*PF	Model OUTFILE for spooled file information.
QSYS/QAFDTAP	*PF	Model OUTFILE for tape file information.
QSYS/QPDSPFD	*PRTF	File description printer file.

Common MONMSG Messages

CPF3011 TYPE not found for file.
CPF3012 File not found.
CPF3014 No file specified can be displayed.
CPF3020 No files have the specified FILEATR.
CPF3021 File not allowed with SYSTEM(*RMT).

CPF3022	SYSTEM(*RMT) not allowed for files.
CPF3030	nn records added to member.
CPF3061	Record format not found.
CPF3064	Library not found.
CPF3067	Error while opening file.
CPF3068	Error while writing to file.
CPF3069	Error while closing file.
CPF3070	Error creating member.
CPF3072	File is a system file.
CPF3074	Not authorized to library.
CPF3075	Library not available.
CPF3076	Error occurred when on display.
CPF3077	Error occurred when canceling display.
CPF3084	Error clearing member.
CPF9851	Overflow value for file too small.
CPF9852	Page size too narrow for file.
CPF9899	Error occurred during processing of command.

...

DSPFFD (Display File Field Description)

Shows field-level information (i.e., a record layout) for a file.

Files Used

QADSPFFD	*PF	Model OUTFILE for field description information.
QPDSPFFD	*PRTF	Field description printer file.

Common MONMSG Messages

CPF3012	File not found.
CPF3014	No file specified can be displayed.
CPF3024	File not allowed.
CPF3052	Description for file not available.
CPF3061	Record format not found for outfile.
CPF3063	Output file not physical file.
CPF3064	Library not found.
CPF3066	Error creating output file.
CPF3067	Error while opening file.
CPF3068	Error while writing to file.
CPF3069	Error while closing file.
CPF3070	Error creating member.
CPF3072	File is a system file.
CPF3074	Not authorized to library.
CPF3075	Library not available.
CPF3076	Error occurred when on display.
CPF3077	Error occurred when canceling display.
CPF3084	Error clearing member.
CPF9851	Overflow value for file too small.
CPF9852	Page size too narrow for file.
CPF9899	Error occurred during processing of command.

...

DSPJOB (Display Job) — *See WRKJOB*
DSPJOBD (Display Job Description) — *See WRKJOBD*

DSPJOBLOG (Display Job Log) — *See also WRKJOB*

Monitors the progress of a job, showing commands and messages related to the job.

Files Used

QSYS/QPJOBLOG	*PRTF	Job log printer file.
QSYS/QPJOBLOGO	*PRTF	Job log printer file for jobs prior to V2R3.

Common MONMSG Messages

CPF0941	Job no longer in system.
CPF1069	End of duplicate names.
CPF1070	Job not found.
CPF2441	Not authorized to display job log.
CPF2443	Job log not displayed or listed because job has ended.
CPF2477	Message queue currently in use.
CPF2523	No job log information.
CPF9847	Error occurred while closing file.

...

DSPLIB (Display Library) — *See WRKLIB*
DSPLIBD (Display Library Description) — *See WRKLIB*
DSPLIBL (Display Library List) — *See CHGLIBL*

DSPLOG (Display Log)

Shows the messages in the system history log.

Files Used

QSYS/QPDSPLOG	*PRTF	Log printer file.

Common MONMSG Messages

CPF2403	Message queue not found.
CPF2447	No entries exist in current version of log.
CPF2478	Not authorized to requested version of log.
CPF2519	Error occurred while processing message ID list.
CPF2537	Too many records written to file.
CPF9847	Error occurred while closing file.

...

DSPMNUA (Display Menu Attributes) — *See WRKMNU*
DSPMOD (Display Module) — *See WRKMOD*

DSPMODSRC (Display Module Source)

Shows the module source display of the ILE source debugger.

MONMSG Messages

(None)

DSPMSG (Display Messages)

Shows the messages in a user message queue or a workstation message queue, and lets you act on them if necessary. You can also use DSPMSG to display and reply to message on the system operator message queue.

Files Used

QSYS/QPDSPMSG	*PRTF	Message display printer file.

Common MONMSG Messages

CPF2203	User profile not correct.
CPF2204	User profile not found.
CPF2217	Not authorized to user profile.

CPF2225	Not able to allocate internal system object.
CPF2401	Not authorized to library.
CPF2403	Message queue not found.
CPF2408	Not authorized to message queue.
CPF2433	Function not allowed for system log message queue.
CPF2450	Work station message queue not allocated to job.
CPF2451	Message queue is allocated to another job.
CPF2477	Message queue currently in use.
CPF2513	Message queue cannot be displayed.
CPF2537	Too many records written to file.
CPF36F7	Message queue QSYSOPR is allocated to another job.
CPF9847	Error occurred while closing file.

...

DSPMSGD (Display Message Descriptions) — *See WRKMSGF*

DSPNETA (Display Network Attributes) — *See CHGNETA*

DSPOBJAUT (Display Object Authority)

EDTOBJAUT (Edit Object Authority)
GRTOBJAUT (Grant Object Authority)
RVKOBJAUT (Revoke Object Authority)

DSPOBJAUT shows a list of authorized users (and authorization lists) for an object, and their authorities. EDTOBJAUT, in addition to listing the authorized users, lets the object owner or the security officer add, change, and remove authority. GRTOBJAUT grants authority to an object, while RVKOBJAUT revokes authority.

Files Used

DSPOBJAUT:

| QSYS/QAOBJAUT | *PF | Model OUTFILE for object authority. |
| QSYS/QPOBJAUT | *PRTF | Object authority printer file. |

Common MONMSG Messages

(All)

CPF2208	Object not found.
CPF2209	Library not found.
CPF2211	Not able to allocate object.
CPF2216	Not authorized to use library.
CPF2283	Authorization list does not exist.

DSPOBJAUT:

CPF2204	User profile not found.
CPF2207	Not authorized to use object.
CPF9843	Object cannot be accessed.
CPF9850	Override of printer file not allowed.
CPF9851	Overflow value for file too small.
CPF9860	Error occurred during output file processing.

...

EDTOBJAUT:

CPF2204	User profile not found.
CPF2207	Not authorized to use object.
CPF2217	Not authorized to user profile.
CPF22B8	Not authorized to change authorities.
CPF22B9	Not authorized to change authorities.

CPF9843   Object cannot be accessed.

GRTOBJAUT:

CPF0601	Not allowed to do operation to file.
CPF0605	Device file saved with storage freed.
CPF0608	Specified user profile not available.
CPF0610	File not available.
CPF2160	Object type not eligible for requested function.
CPF2207	Not authorized to use object.
CPF2210	Operation not allowed for object type.
CPF2223	Not authorized to give authority to object.
CPF2227	One or more errors occurred during processing of command.
CPF2253	No objects found.
CPF2254	No libraries found.
CPF2273	Authority may not have been changed.
CPF2290	*EXCLUDE cannot be specified with another authority.
CPF22DA	Operation on file not allowed.
CPF3202	File in use.
CPF3203	Cannot allocate object for file.
CPF323C	QRECOVERY library could not be allocated.
CPF3252	Maximum number of machine locks exceeded.
CPF326A	Operation not successful for file.

...

RVKOBJAUT:

CPF0601	Not allowed to do operation to file.
CPF0605	Device file saved with storage freed.
CPF0608	Specified user profile not available.
CPF0610	File not available.
CPF2160	Object type not eligible for requested function.
CPF2204	User profile not found.
CPF2207	Not authorized to use object.
CPF2210	Operation not allowed for object type.
CPF2223	Not authorized to give authority to object.
CPF2224	Not authorized to revoke authority for object.
CPF2227	One or more errors occurred during processing of command.
CPF2253	No objects found.
CPF2254	No libraries found.
CPF2256	Specified authority for the object not revoked from all users.
CPF2273	Authority may not have been changed.
CPF22DA	Operation on file not allowed.
CPF3202	File in use.
CPF3203	Cannot allocate object for file.
CPF326A	Operation not successful for file.

...

DSPOBJD (Display Object Description) — See WRKOBJ

DSPOVR (Display Override) — See also DLTOVR, OVRDBF, OVRDSPF, OVRMSGF, OVRPRTF, OVRSAVF

Shows active file overrides at a call level.

Files Used

QSYS/QPDSPOVR   *PRTF   Overrides printer file.

MONMSG Messages

CPF9842   Overrides not found for file.
CPF9847   Error occurred while closing file.
CPF9850   Override of printer file not allowed.
CPF9851   Overflow value for file too small.
CPF9852   Page size too narrow for file.

DSPPFM (Display Physical File Member) — *See CRTPF*
DSPPGM (Display Program) — *See WRKPGM*
DSPPGMADP (Display Programs that Adopt)

Checks for security exposures, by showing objects that adopt the authority of a specific user profile.

Files Used

QSYS/QADPGMAD	*PF	Model OUTFILE for program adoption.
QSYS/QPPGMADP	*PRTF	Program adoption printer file.

MONMSG Messages

CPF2204   User profile not found.
CPF2213   Not able to allocate user profile.
CPF2217   Not authorized to user profile.
CPF9850   Override of printer file not allowed.
CPF9860   Error occurred during output file processing.

DSPPGMREF (Display Program References)

Lists the objects to which one or more programs refer.

Files Used

QSYS/QADSPPGM	*PF	Model OUTFILE for program references.
QSYS/QPDSPPGM	*PRTF	Program reference printer file.

MONMSG Messages

CPF3033   Object not found.
CPF3034   Object not displayed.
CPF3052   Description for file not available.
CPF3061   Record format not found.
CPF3063   Output file not physical file.
CPF3064   Library not found.
CPF3066   Error creating output file.
CPF3067   Error while opening file.
CPF3068   Error while writing to file.
CPF3069   Error while closing file.
CPF3070   Error creating member.
CPF3072   File is a system file.
CPF3074   Not authorized to library.
CPF3075   Library not available.
CPF3076   Error occurred when on display.
CPF3077   Error occurred when canceling display.
CPF3084   Error clearing member.

DSPPGMVAR (Display Program Variable) — *See STRDBG*
DSPRCDLCK (Display Record Locks) — *See WRKOBJLCK*
DSPSAVF (Display Save File) — *See CRTSAVF*
DSPSBSD (Display Subsystem Description) — *See WRKSBS*
DSPSPLF (Display Spooled File) — *See WRKSPLF*

DSPSRVPGM (Display Service Program) — *See WRKSRVPGM*

DSPSYSSTS (Display System Status) — *See WRKSYSSTS*

DSPSYSVAL (Display System Value) — *See WRKSYSVAL*

DSPTAP (Display Tape)

Shows information about the files on a magnetic tape. In addition to volume and data file label information, DSPTAP can show information about objects that have been saved on the tape.

Files Used

QSYS/QPTAPDSP	*PRTF	Printer file for OUTPUT(*PRINT).
QSYS/QPSRODSP	*PRTF	Save/restore printer file.

MONMSG Messages

CPF3704	Request ended; data management error occurred.
CPF3743	File cannot be restored, displayed, or listed.
CPF3793	Machine storage limit reached.
CPF6708	Command ended due to error.
CPF6718	Cannot allocate device.
CPF6721	Device not a tape device.
CPF6723	File not found on tape.
CPF6724	File label not found on tape.
CPF6751	Load failure occurred.
CPF6760	Device not ready.
CPF6772	Volume cannot be processed.
CPF9814	Device not found.
CPF9825	Not authorized to device.
CPF9847	Error occurred while closing file.
CPF9850	Override of printer file not allowed.
CPF9851	Overflow value for file too small.

DSPTRC (Display Trace) — *See STRDBG*

DSPTRCDTA (Display Trace Data) — *See STRDBG*

DSPUSRPRF (Display User Profile) — *See WRKUSRPRF*

DUPDKT (Duplicate Diskette)

Copies the contents of a diskette to one or more diskettes.

MONMSG Messages

CPF5102	Permanent I/O error.
CPF6151	Cannot duplicate diskette.
CPF6157	Duplicate diskette ended; previous error occurred.
CPF6716	Device not a diskette device.
CPF6718	Cannot allocate device.
CPF9814	Device not found.
CPF9825	Not authorized to device.

DUPTAP (Duplicate Tape)

Copies the contents of a tape to one or more tapes.

MONMSG Messages

CPF6708	Command ended due to error.
CPF6718	Cannot allocate device.
CPF6720	Incorrect volume found.
CPF6721	Device not a tape device.
CPF6722	End of tape found.
CPF6740	TODEV and FROMDEV must be different.
CPF6741	Nonlabeled tape format not valid.
CPF6751	Load failure occurred.

CPF6754 Active file found on volume.
CPF6760 Device not ready.
CPF6768 Volume is write protected.
CPF6772 Volume cannot be processed.
CPF9814 Device not found.
CPF9825 Not authorized to device.

EDTAUTL (Edit Authorization List) — *See WRKAUTL*
EDTLIBL (Edit Library List) — *See CHGLIBL*
EDTOBJAUT (Edit Object Authority) — *See DSPOBJAUT*
ELSE (Else) — *See IF*
ENDCPYSCN (End Copy Screen) — *See STRCPYSCN*
ENDDBG (End Debug) — *See STRDBG*
ENDDO (End Do) — *See DO*
ENDGRPJOB (End Group Job) — *See TFRGRPJOB*
ENDJOB (End Job) — *See WRKJOB*
ENDJOBABN (End Job Abnormal) — *See WRKJOB*
ENDPGM (End Program) — *See PGM*
ENDRCV (End Receive) — *See RCVF*

ENDRQS (End Request)

Cancels a previously requested command. This command is also invoked by option 2 on the System Request menu, available by pressing SysRq.

MONMSG Messages
(None)

ENDSBS (End Subsystem) — *See WRKSBS*
ENDWTR (End Writer) — *See WRKWTR*

GOTO (Go To)

Branches from one part of a CL program to another.

MONMSG Messages
(None)

GRTOBJAUT (Grant Object Authority) — *See DSPOBJAUT*

GRTUSRAUT (Grant User Authority)

Grants authority to a user by referring to another user.

MONMSG Messages
CPF2204 User profile not found.
CPF2211 Not able to allocate object.
CPF2213 Not able to allocate user profile.
CPF2217 Not authorized to user profile.
CPF2222 Storage limit is greater than specified for user profile.
CPF2223 Not authorized to give authority to object.
CPF2252 Authority given to nn objects. Authority not given to nn objects.

HLDJOB (Hold Job) — *See WRKJOB*
HLDJOBQ (Hold Job Queue) — *See WRKJOBQ*
HLDJOBSCDE (Hold Job Schedule Entry) — *See WRKJOBSCDE*
HLDOUTQ (Hold Output Queue) — *See WRKOUTQ*
HLDSPLF (Hold Spooled File) — *See WRKSPLF*
HLDWTR (Hold Writer) — *See WRKWTR*

IF (If)
ELSE (Else)
IF evaluates an expression, conditionally processing a CL command (or DO group of commands) if the expression is true. ELSE can follow an IF command (or its DO group); if the expression is not true, the command (or DO group) associated with the ELSE command will execute.

MONMSG Messages

ELSE:
(None)

IF:
CPF0816   %SWITCH mask &1 not valid.

INZDKT (Initialize Diskette)
Initializes (formats) a diskette, so that it can be used by the system.

MONMSG Messages
CPF6156   Cancel reply received for message.
CPF6716   Device not a diskette device.
CPF6717   Initialize diskette ended; previous errors occurred.
CPF6718   Cannot allocate device.
CPF6757   Owner identifier contains wrong characters.
CPF6758   Volume identifier contains wrong characters.
CPF6779   Format (FMT) specified for diskette not valid.
CPF9814   Device not found.
CPF9825   Not authorized to device.

INZPFM (Initialize Physical File Member) — See CRTPF

INZTAP (Initialize Tape)
Initializes (formats) a tape, so that it can be used by the system.

MONMSG Messages
CPF6702   Error processing volume.
CPF6708   Command ended due to error.
CPF6715   Error at beginning of tape.
CPF6718   Cannot allocate device.
CPF6720   Incorrect volume found.
CPF6721   Device not a tape device.
CPF6722   End of tape found.
CPF6750   NEWVOL(*NONE) not valid for device.
CPF6751   Load failure occurred.
CPF6754   Active file found.
CPF6760   Device not ready.
CPF6762   Wrong type of cartridge.
CPF6763   Wrong type of cartridge.
CPF6768   Volume is write protected.
CPF6772   Volume cannot be processed.
CPF6774   New volume is a nonstandard labeled tape. Volume not prepared.
CPF9814   Device not found.
CPF9825   Not authorized to device.

LODRUN (Load and Run Media Program)
Restores a program called QINSTAPP from a tape or diskette, then executes the program. This command is useful for implementing a single command installation of an application.

MONMSG Messages
(None)

MONMSG (Monitor Message)
Monitors for escape, notify, and status messages sent to a program's program message queue. If a MONMSG appears at the beginning of a program (immediately following the declarations), it is in effect for the entire program. If a MONMSG appears anywhere else, it is in effect only for the command immediately preceding it.

MONMSG Messages
(None)

MOVOBJ (Move Object) — *See also CHKOBJ, CPROBJ, CRTDUPOBJ, DMPOBJ, RNMOBJ, SAVOBJ, WRKOBJ, WRKOBJLCK*
Moves an object from one library to another.

Common MONMSG Messages
CPF0601	Not allowed to do operation to file.
CPF0602	File already in library.
CPF0605	Device file saved with storage freed.
CPF0610	File not available.
CPF0678	Operation not performed for file.
CPF1763	Cannot allocate one or more libraries.
CPF2105	Object not found.
CPF2110	Library not found.
CPF2112	Object already exists.
CPF2113	Cannot allocate library.
CPF2114	Cannot allocate object.
CPF2135	Object already exists in library.
CPF2150	Object information function failed.
CPF2151	Operation failed.
CPF2160	Object type not eligible for requested function.
CPF2182	Not authorized to library.
CPF2183	Object cannot be moved into library.
CPF2189	Not authorized to object.
CPF2193	Object cannot be moved into library.
CPF22BC	Object is not program defined.
CPF2512	Operation not allowed for message queue.
CPF3201	File already exists.
CPF3202	File in use.
CPF3203	Cannot allocate object.
CPF320B	Operation was not valid for database file.
CPF320C	File not allowed in SQL collection.
CPF3220	Cannot do operation on file.
CPF322D	Operation not done for data base file.
CPF3231	Cannot move file from library.
CPF323C	QRECOVERY library could not be allocated.
CPF323D	User does not have correct authority.
CPF324B	Cannot allocate dictionary for file.
CPF324C	Concurrent authority holder operation prevents move, rename or restore.
CPF325D	Field CCSID values not compatible.
CPF327C	File cannot be moved into library.
CPF3323	Job queue already exists.
CPF3330	Necessary resource not available.

CPF3353	Output queue already exists.
CPF3373	Job queue not moved. Job queue in use.
CPF3374	Output queue not moved. Output queue in use.
CPF3467	Output queue deleted and then created again.
CPF3469	Operation not allowed for output queue.
CPF7010	Object already exists.
CPF7014	Object cannot be moved to library.
CPF9827	Object cannot be created in library.

...

MRGMSGF (Merge Message File)

Merges messages from one message file with those in another.

Common MONMSG Messages

CPF2401	Not authorized to library.
CPF2407	Message file not found.
CPF2411	Not authorized to message file.
CPF2452	Replaced message file must contain no messages.
CPF2461	Message file could not be extended.
CPF2483	Message file currently in use.
CPF2519	Error occurred while processing message ID list.
CPF2561	Messages were not merged.
CPF2562	Cannot specify the same message file more than once.
CPF9838	User profile storage limit exceeded.

...

OPNDBF (Open Database File) — *See also OPNQRYF*

CLOF (Close File)

OPNDBF opens a database file member, for later processing. CLOF closes a file that had been opened by the OPNDBF or OPNQRYF command.

MONMSG Messages

CLOF:

CPF4519	Member not closed.
CPF4520	No file open with identifier.

OPNDBF:

CPF4125	Open of member failed.
CPF4152	Error opening member.
CPF4174	OPNID for file already exists.
CPF4175	Output only and MBR(*ALL) cannot be used together.
CPF4176	File not a data base file.
CPF8367	Cannot perform commitment control operation.

OPNQRYF (Open Query File) — *See also CPYFRMQRYF, OPNDBF*

Opens a file that contains a set of records satisfying a database query request. High-level language programs can then access the records in the file. OPNQRYF is commonly used to select a subset of the records in a file, or to sort the records in the file. While CL cannot directly process records from an OPNQRYF command, the CPYFRMQRYF can copy the records into a database file for later processing.

Common MONMSG Messages

CPF4174	OPNID for file already exists.

CPF9801	Object not found.
CPF9802	Not authorized to object.
CPF9812	File not found.
CPF9813	Record format not found.
CPF9815	Member not found.
CPF9820	Not authorized to use library.
CPF9822	Not authorized to file.
CPF9826	Cannot allocate file.
CPF9899	Error occurred during processing of command.
CPI4011	Query running. nn records selected, nn processed.
CPI4301	Query running.
CPI4302	Query running. Building access path for file.
CPI4303	Query running. Creating copy of file.
CPI4304	Query running. nn records selected. Selection complete.
CPI4305	Query running. Sorting copy of file.
CPI4306	Query running. Building access path from file.

...

OVRDBF (Override with Database File)

Redirects processing from a physical, logical, or DDM file named in a program to another file or file member, or temporarily overrides certain properties of the file to meet specific processing requirements. The override will be in effect only at the current call level, and any subsequent call levels.

MONMSG Messages

(None)

OVRDSPF (Override with Display File)

Redirects processing from a display file named in a program to another file, or temporarily overrides certain attributes of the file to meet specific processing requirements. The override will be in effect only at the current call level, and any subsequent call levels.

MONMSG Messages

(None)

OVRMSGF (Override with Message File)

Redirects processing from a message file named in a program to another message file to meet specific processing requirements. The program will use messages from the overriding file; if a message does not exist in the overriding file, the message from the overridden file will be used instead. The override will be in effect only at the current call level, and any subsequent call levels.

MONMSG Messages

(None)

OVRPRTF (Override with Printer File)

Redirects processing from a printer device file name in a program to another printer file, or temporarily overrides certain properties of the file to meet specific processing requirements. The override will be in effect only at the current call level, and any subsequent call levels. OVRPRTF is typically used to hold a spooled report, to change the defined page size, or to place the report on a specific output queue.

MONMSG Messages
CPF7343   Channel number specified more than once on
              CHLVAL.

OVRSAVF (Override with Save File)
Redirects an online save file named in a program to another file, or
temporarily overrides certain attributes of the save file. The override is
effective at the current call level, and any subsequent call levels. The
save/restore commands will not recognize any overrides.

MONMSG Messages
(None)

PGM (Program)
ENDPGM (End Program)
PGM marks the beginning of a CL program, and optionally names the
CL variables which will hold the parameters to be passed to the program.
ENDPGM marks the end of a CL program.

MONMSG Messages
(None)

POSDBF (Position Database File)
Positions the file cursor of an open database file to the beginning or end.

MONMSG Messages
CPF5213   Positioning of member failed.
CPF5230   No file open with OPNID.

PRTDEVADR (Print Device Addresses)
Prints a report of addresses of twinaxial devices attached to a local
workstation controller.

Files Used
QSYS/QPDDEVA   *PRTF   Device address printer file.

Common MONMSG Messages
CPF2602   Controller not found.
CPF2625   Not able to allocate object.
CPF2628   Device description previously deleted.
CPF2634   Not authorized to object.
CPF263B   Controller not a local work station controller.
CPF9850   Override of printer file not allowed.
...

PRTDSKINF (Print Disk Information) — See RTVDSKINF

PWRDWNSYS (Power Down System)
Powers down the system, then optionally restarts it from one of three IPL
sources. The IPL sources are:
A   Permanent PTF memory area
B   Temporary PTF memory area
C   Tape device

Common MONMSG Messages
CPF1036   System powering down with *CNTRLD option.
CPF1037   System powering down with *IMMED option.
CPF1038   No authority to use command.
...

RCLACTGRP (Reclaim Activation Group)
Frees the resources associated with an activation group. An activation group is a means of partitioning a job and allocating resources within that job substructure.

MONMSG Messages
CPF1653   Activation group not found.
CPF1654   Activation group cannot be deleted.

RCLRSC (Reclaim Resources)
Frees storage and closes files left open by programs in a job that have ended abnormally. It is normally used in an "application driver" CL program to ensure that any resources used by the application are freed when the application ends.

MONMSG Messages
(None)

RCLSPLSTG (Reclaim Spool Storage)
Frees spooled file storage that has not been used for a specified number of days, deleting unused spooled file database members.

MONMSG Messages
(None)

RCLSTG (Reclaim Storage)
Cleans up disk storage, correcting abnormal conditions that may have occurred as the result of unexpected failures. These conditions might include damaged objects, objects without owners, or objects authorized by a damaged authorization list, among others. This command requires that the system be reduced to a restricted condition.

Files Used
QSYS/QPRCLDMP   *PRTF   Reclaim dump listing.

Common MONMSG Messages
CPF2119   Library locked.
CPF2120   Cannot delete library.
CPF2126   Attempt to recover library failed.
CPF8204   Commitment control cannot be active during reclaim storage.
CPF8209   System not in proper state to reclaim storage.
CPF8224   Duplicate object found while moving or renaming member.
CPI8206   nn% of objects processed.
CPI8210   Processing data base relationships.
CPI8212   Data base/library recovery in progress.
CPI8213   Processing objects on the system.
CPI8214   All permanent objects have valid owners.
CPI8215   Object description verification in progress.
CPI8216   Final clean up in progress.
...

RCVF (Receive File)
ENDRCV (End Receive)
SNDF (Send File)
SNDRCVF (Send/Receive File)
WAIT (Wait)

With these commands, a CL program can read data from a database file, or can write a formatted display onto a workstation, then read the user's typed responses. CL programs cannot write data to a database file. RCVF reads a record from a database or display file.

SNDF writes a record format to a display. SNDRCVF writes a record format to a display, then reads the user's response. WAIT accepts input from the display when a previous RCVF or SNDRCVF command does not wait for the input. ENDRCV cancels a request for input when a previous RCVF or SNDRCVF command does not wait for input.

Common MONMSG Messages

(All except ENDRCV, WAIT)

CPF0861	File not a display file.
CPF0864	End of file detected.
CPF4101	File not found or inline data file missing.

...

ENDRCV:

CPF0883	*FILE not valid in DEV parameter for file.
CPF4101	File not found or inline data file missing.

RCVF:

CPF0860	File not a data base file.
CPF0865	File has more than one record format.

...

SNDF:

CPF0887	Data available from previous input request.
	SNDRCVF:
CPF0887	Data available from previous input request.

...

WAIT:

CPF0882	No corresponding RCVF or SNDRCVF command for WAIT command.
CPF0888	Command not run because job being ended.
CPF0889	No data available for input request within specified time.
CPF4101	File not found or inline data file missing.

...

RCVMSG (Receive Message) — *See also SNDMSG*

Receives a message being sent to a message queue, copying the message and its properties into CL program variables.

Common MONMSG Messages

CPF2401	Not authorized to library.
CPF2403	Message queue not found.
CPF2408	Not authorized to message queue.
CPF2410	Message key not found in message queue.
CPF2415	End of requests.
CPF2450	Work station message queue not allocated to job.
CPF2451	Message queue is allocated to another job.
CPF2471	Length of field not valid.
CPF2477	Message queue currently in use.
CPF2479	Call stack entry not found.
CPF247A	Call stack entry not found.
CPF2482	Message type not valid.

CPF2551   Message key and message type combination not valid.
CPF36F7   Message queue QSYSOPR is allocated to another job.
...

RETURN (Return)
Ends a CL program, returning control to the calling program.

MONMSG Messages
CPF2415   End of requests.

RGZPFM (Reorganize Physical File Member) — *See CRTPF*
RLSJOB (Release Job) — *See WRKJOB*
RLSJOBQ (Release Job Queue) — *See WRKJOBQ*
RLSJOBSCDE (Release Job Schedule Entry) — *See WRKJOBSCDE*
RLSOUTQ (Release Output Queue) — *See WRKOUTQ*
RLSSPLF (Release Spooled File) — *See WRKSPLF*
RLSWTR (Release Writer) — *See WRKWTR*
RMVAUTLE (Remove Authorization List Entry) — *See WRKAUTL*
RMVBKP (Remove Breakpoint) — *See STRDBG*
RMVBNDDIRE (Remove Binding Directory Entry) — *See WRKBNDDIR*
RMVDIRE (Remove Directory Entry) — *See WRKDIR*
RMVJOBQE (Remove Job Queue Entry) — *See WRKSBSD*
RMVJOBSCDE (Remove Job Schedule Entry) — *See WRKJOBSCDE*
RMVLIBLE (Remove Library List Entry) — *See CHGLIBL*

RMVM (Remove Member)
Removes one or more members from a physical or logical file, deleting any data in the member, and freeing its storage.

MONMSG Messages
CPF3203   Cannot allocate object.
CPF320A   Member cannot be removed.
CPF320B   Operation was not valid for database file.
CPF3220   Cannot do operation.
CPF3273   File or member not created, deleted or changed.
CPF7301   nn members not removed.
CPF7310   Member not removed.

RMVMSG (Remove Message)
Removes one or more messages from a message queue.

Common MONMSG Messages
CPF2401   Not authorized to library.
CPF2403   Message queue not found.
CPF2408   Not authorized to message queue.
CPF2410   Message key not found in message queue.
CPF2450   Work station message queue not allocated to job.
CPF2477   Message queue currently in use.
CPF2479   Call stack entry not found.
CPF247A   Call stack entry not found.
CPF9838   User profile storage limit exceeded.
...

RMVMSGD (Remove Message Description) — *See WRKMSGF*

RMVPGM (Remove Program) — *See STRDBG*
RMVRPYLE (Remove Reply List Entry) — *See WRKRPYLE*
RMVTRC (Remove Trace) — *See STRDBG*
RNMDIRE (Rename Directory Entry) — *See WRKDIR*

RNMM (Rename Member)
Renames a file member.

MONMSG Messages
CPF3178   Member not renamed.
CPF3220   Cannot do operation on file.

RNMOBJ (Rename Object) — *See also CHKOBJ, CPROBJ, CRTDUPOBJ, DMPOBJ, MOVOBJ, SAVOBJ, WRKOBJ, WRKOBJLCK*
Renames an object.

Common MONMSG Messages
CPF0601   Not allowed to do operation to file.
CPF0602   File already in library.
CPF0605   Device file saved with storage freed.
CPF0610   File not available.
CPF0678   Operation not performed for file.
CPF1763   Cannot allocate one or more libraries.
CPF2105   Object not found.
CPF2110   Library not found.
CPF2111   Library already exists.
CPF2112   Object already exists.
CPF2113   Cannot allocate library.
CPF2114   Cannot allocate object.
CPF2132   Object already exists.
CPF2136   Renaming library failed.
CPF2139   Rename of library failed.
CPF2140   Rename of library previously failed.
CPF2150   Object information function failed.
CPF2151   Operation failed.
CPF2160   Object type not eligible for requested function.
CPF2164   Rename of library not complete.
CPF2182   Not authorized to library.
CPF2189   Not authorized to object.
CPF2691   Rename of object did not complete.
CPF2692   Object must be varied off.
CPF2693   Name cannot be used for rename.
CPF2694   Object cannot be renamed.
CPF2696   Object not renamed.
CPF3201   File already exists.
CPF3202   File in use.
CPF3203   Cannot allocate object for file.
CPF320B   Operation was not valid for database file.
CPF3220   Cannot do operation on file.
CPF322D   Operation not done for data base file.
CPF323D   User does not have correct authority.
CPF324C   Concurrent authority holder operation prevents move, rename or restore.
CPF3323   Job queue already exists.
CPF3330   Necessary resource not available.
CPF3353   Output queue already exists.

CPF3375   Job queue not renamed. Job queue in use.
CPF3376   Output queue not renamed. Output queue in use.
CPF3467   Output queue deleted and then created again.
CPF3469   Operation not allowed for output queue.
CPF8D05   Library already exists.
CPF9809   Library cannot be accessed.
CPF9827   Object cannot be created.
...

RSMBKP (Resume Breakpoint) — *See STRDBG*
RSTAUT (Restore Authority) — *See SAVSECDTA*
RSTCFG (Restore Configuration) — *See SAVCFG*
RSTDLO (Restore Document Library Object) — *See SAVDLO*
RSTLIB (Restore Library) — *See SAVLIB*
RSTLICPGM (Restore Licensed Program) — *See SAVLICPGM*
RSTOBJ (Restore Object) — *See SAVOBJ*
RSTUSRPRF (Restore User Profiles) — *See SAVSECDTA*
RTVAUTLE (Retrieve Authorization List Entry) — *See WRKAUTL*

RTVCFGSRC (Retrieve Configuration Source)
Builds the CL source necessary to create existing configuration objects, such as lines, controllers, and devices.

MONMSG Messages
CPF2207   Not authorized to use object.
CPF263E   File member contains its maximum sequence number.
CPF263F   No objects found.
CPF264A   Record length is too small.
CPF264C   Source file member not found.
CPF9820   Not authorized to use library.
CPF9847   Error occurred while closing file.
CPF9848   Cannot open file member.
CPF9849   Error while processing file member.

RTVCFGSTS (Retrieve Configuration Status) — See
WRKCFGSTS

RTVCLSRC (Retrieve CL Source)
"Decompiles" a CL source program, retrieving the source originally used to compile the program.

MONMSG Messages
CPF0560   Program not a CL program.
CPF0561   Unable to retrieve CL source.
CPF0562   File not a data base source file.
CPF0563   Record length too small for data base source file.
CPF0564   Unable to add data base member.
CPF0565   Source not retrieved.
CPF0566   Source not available.
CPF9801   Object not found.
CPF9806   Cannot perform function for object.
CPF9809   Library cannot be accessed.
CPF9811   Program not found.
CPF9820   Not authorized to use library.
CPF9821   Not authorized to program.
CPF9822   Not authorized to file.
CPF9848   Cannot open file.

CPF9849   Error while processing file member.

RTVDSKINF (Retrieve Disk Information)

PRTDSKINF (Print Disk Information)

RTVDSKINF collects disk space usage information, storing it in database file QUSRSYS/QAEZDISK, member QCURRENT. PRTDSKINF prints one or more disk space usage reports using the collected information.

Files Used

PRTDSKINF:

QSYS/QAEZDISK	*PF	Database file of disk information.
QSYS/QPEZDISK	*PRTF	Disk information report printer file.

MONMSG Messages

(All)

CPF1E99   Unexpected error occurred.
CPF1ED1   Not authorized to collect disk space information.
CPF1ED2   File QAEZDISK is in use and cannot be accessed.

PRTDSKINF:

CPF1ED0   Current collection of disk space information not found.
CPF1EEC   Not authorized to file QAEZDISK.

RTVDTAARA (Retrieve Data Area) — *See WRKDTAARA*
RTVGRPA (Retrieve Group Attributes) — *See CHGGRPA*
RTVJOBA (Retrieve Job Attributes) — *See WRKJOB*
RTVLIBD (Retrieve Library Description) — *See WRKLIB*

RTVMBRD (Retrieve Member Description)

Retrieves information about file member(s), placing the information into CL program variables. The parameters that you use to retrieve the information are listed below:

ACCPTHSIZ	*DEC (12 0)	Access path size in bytes.
CHGDATE	*CHAR 13	Date changed (CYYMMDDHHMMSS).
CRTDATE	*CHAR 13	Date created (CYYMMDDHHMMSS).
DTASPCSIZ	*DEC (15 0)	Data space size in bytes.
EXPDATE	*CHAR 7	Member expiration date (CYYMMDD).
FILEATR	*CHAR 3	File attribute: *PF, *LF.
FILETYPE	*CHAR 5	File type: *DATA, *SRC.
NBRCURRCD	*DEC (10 0)	Number of nondeleted records.
NBRDLTRCD	*DEC (10 0)	Number of deleted records.
NBRDTAMBRS	*DEC (2 0)	Number of data members for a logical file member.
RESETDATE	*CHAR 7	Date the USEDATE and USECOUNT were reset (CYYMMDD).
RSTDATE	*CHAR 13	Date restored (CYYMMDDHHMMSS).
RTNLIB	*CHAR 10	Library name.

RTNMBR	*CHAR 10	Member name.
RTNSYSTEM	*CHAR 4	System: *LCL, *RMT.
SAVDATE	*CHAR 13	Date saved (CYYMMDDHHMMSS).
SHARE	*CHAR 4	Shared open data path status: *YES, *NO.
SRCCHGDATE	*CHAR 13	Last source change date (CYYMMDDHHMMSS).
SRCTYPE	*CHAR 10	Source type.
TEXT	*CHAR 50	Member text.
USECOUNT	*DEC (5 0)	Number of days the objects has been used.
USEDATE	*CHAR 7	Last date used (CYYMMDD).

Common MONMSG Messages

CPF3018	Member not available.
CPF3019	File has no members.
CPF3027	File not a database file.
CPF3038	Attributes for return variable not valid.
CPF3039	Return variable too small to hold result.
CPF3049	*NEXT or *PRV member does not exist.
CPF3051	File not available.
CPF325F	Conversion of the text failed.
CPF327B	File information cannot be retrieved.
CPF9806	Cannot perform function for object,
CPF9812	File not found.
CPF9815	Member not found.
CPF9820	Not authorized to use library.
CPF9822	Not authorized to file.
...	

RTVMSG (Retrieve Message) — *See WRKMSGF*
RTVNETA (Retrieve Network Attributes) — *See CHGNETA*
RTVOBJD (Retrieve Object Description) — *See CHGOBJD*
RTVSYSVAL (Retrieve System Value) — *See WRKSYSVAL*
RTVUSRPRF (Retrieve User Profile) — *See WRKUSRPRF*
RVKOBJAUT (Revoke Object Authority) — *See DSPOBJAUT*

SAVCFG (Save Configuration) — *See also SAVSTG, SAVSYS*
RSTCFG (Restore Configuration)
These commands are used to save and restore configuration objects, such as line descriptions, controller descriptions, and device descriptions. SAVCFG saves the information to offline media or an online save file. RSTCFG restores the information to the system.

Files Used

RSTCFG:

QSYS/QASRRSTO	*PF	Model OUTFILE for configuration.
QSYS/QPSRLDSP	*PRTF	Restored objects printer file.

SAVCFG:

QSYS/QASAVOBJ	*PF	Model OUTFILE for saved objects.
QSYS/QPSAVOBJ	*PRTF	Save objects printer file.

Common MONMSG Messages

(All)

CPF3709	Tape devices do not support same densities.
CPF3727	Duplicate device specified in device name list.
CPF3728	Diskette device specified with other devices.
CPF3767	Device not found.
CPF3768	Device not valid for command.
CPF3782	File not a save file.
CPF3793	Machine storage limit reached.
CPF3794	Save or restore operation ended unsuccessfully.
CPF3795	Error while processing.
CPF3812	Save file in use.
CPF5729	Not able to allocate object.
CPF9809	Library cannot be accessed.
CPF9812	File not found.
...	

RSTCFG:

CPF3707	Save file contains no data.
CPF370C	Not authorized to ALWOBJDIF parameter.
CPF3743	File cannot be restored, displayed, or listed.
CPF3769	File found on media not save/restore file.
CPF376B	File not found.
CPF377B	No objects restored. nn objects excluded.
CPF377C	nn objects restored; nn not restored; nn excluded.
CPF3780	Specified file for library not found.
CPF3791	End of file.
CPF3796	Storage limit exceeded for user profile.
CPF379B	Objects from save file not restored.
CPF3805	Objects from save file not restored.
CPF3807	Data decompression error for save file.
CPF9820	Not authorized to use library.
CPF9822	Not authorized to file.
CPF9825	Not authorized to device.
...	

SAVCFG:

CPF3731	Cannot use object.
CPF3737	Save and restore data area not found.
CPF376D	Not all configuration objects saved to save file.
CPF376E	Not all configuration objects saved.
CPF3894	Cancel reply received for message.
CPF9847	Error occurred while closing file.
CPF9850	Override of printer file not allowed.
CPF9851	Overflow value for file too small.
CPF9860	Error occurred during output file processing.

SAVCHGOBJ (Save Changed Object) — *See SAVOBJ*

SAVDLO (Save Document Library Object)

RSTDLO (Restore Document Library Object)

These commands save and restore documents, folders, and mail.
SAVDLO saves the objects to offline media or an online save file.
RSTDLO restores the objects to the system.

Files Used

RSTDLO:

QSYS/QAOJRSTO	*PF	Model OUTFILE for restored document library objects.
QSYS/QPRSTDLO	*PRTF	Restored documents and folders printer file.

SAVDLO:

QSYS/QAOJSAVO	*PF	Model OUTFILE for saved document library objects.
QSYS/QPSAVDLO	*PRTF	Saved document library objects printer file.

Common MONMSG Messages

(All)

CPF3728	Diskette device specified with other devices.
CPF3767	Device not found.
CPF3812	Save file in use.
CPF908A	Requester not enrolled.
CPF9812	File not found.
CPF9820	Not authorized to use library.
CPF9822	Not authorized to file.
CPF9825	Not authorized to device.
CPF9850	Override of printer file not allowed.
CPF9851	Overflow value for file too small.
CPF9860	Error occurred during output file processing.
CPF9899	Error occurred during processing of command.

...

RSTDLO:

CPF370C	Not authorized to ALWOBJDIF parameter.
CPF3718	Restore command not valid for file.
CPF3780	Specified file for library not found.
CPF3782	File not a save file.
CPF9003	nn document library objects restored. nn not restored.
CPF9069	User not permitted to restore into folder.
CPF909B	nn document library objects restored. nn not restored.
CPF90B4	nn folders restored to system, nn not restored.
CPF90CD	Not authorized to restore distributions.
CPF90E0	Not enough authority for ALWOBJDIF(*ALL).
CPF90E7	Document library objects not restored.
CPF9412	List of folder names not allowed with DLO parameter.

...

SAVDLO:

CPF3768	Device not valid for command.
CPF3793	Machine storage limit reached.
CPF3795	Error while processing.
CPF9006	User not enrolled in system distribution directory.
CPF902E	nn document library objects saved. nn not saved.
CPF9030	Owner profile not found.

CPF903B	Too many objects for save file.
CPF903C	No document library objects saved.
CPF9046	No documents found satisfying search specification in folder.
CPF9053	Not authorized to requested function.
CPF9056	Not authorized to requested function.
CPF906B	No document library objects saved.
CPF90B2	List of folder names not valid with DLO parameter.
CPF90C1	Document list empty.
CPF90C2	Document list not used.
CPF90D7	Documents not saved.
CPF90E1	Folder cannot be used with TGTRLS(*PRV).
CPF90E5	Not authorized to document list.
CPF9410	nn document library objects saved. nn not saved.

...

SAVLIB (Save Library)

RSTLIB (Restore Library)

The commands save and restore the entire contents of one or more libraries. SAVLIB saves one or more libraries to offline media, or a single library to an online save file. RSTLIB restores one or more libraries to the system.

Files Used

RSTLIB:

QSYS/QASRRSTO	*PF	Model OUTFILE for libraries.
QSYS/QPSRLDSP	*PRTF	Restored objects printer file.

SAVLIB:

QSYS/QASAVOBJ	*PF	Model OUTFILE for saved objects.
QSYS/QPSAVOBJ	*PRTF	Saved objects printer file.

Common MONMSG Messages

(All)

CPF3709	Tape devices do not support same densities.
CPF3727	Duplicate device specified in device name list.
CPF3728	Diskette device specified with other devices.
CPF3730	Not authorized to object.
CPF3731	Cannot use object.
CPF3767	Device not found.
CPF3768	Device not valid for command.
CPF3770	No objects saved or restored for library.
CPF3781	Library not found.
CPF3782	File not a save file.
CPF3785	Not all subsystems ended.
CPF3793	Machine storage limit reached.
CPF3794	Save or restore operation ended unsuccessfully.
CPF3795	Error while processing.
CPF3812	Save file in use.
CPF3818	Starting library not found.
CPF3894	Cancel reply received for message.
CPF5729	Not able to allocate object.

CPF9809 Library cannot be accessed.
CPF9812 File not found.
CPF9820 Not authorized to library.
CPF9822 Not authorized to file.
CPF9825 Not authorized to device.

...

RSTLIB:
CPF3705 Object not journaled.
CPF3706 Object not restored.
CPF3707 Save file contains no data.
CPF370C Not authorized to ALWOBJDIF parameter.
CPF372C Library not restored to ASP.
CPF3732 Object status changed during restore operation.
CPF373E Library not restored to ASP.
CPF3740 Object not found.
CPF3743 File cannot be restored, displayed, or listed.
CPF3752 No record of save operation exists for library.
CPF3757 Object not restored.
CPF3758 Object not restored.
CPF375F File not selected. Cannot restore from save type.
CPF3769 File found on media not save/restore file.
CPF376B File not found.
CPF3773 nn objects restored. nn not restored.
CPF3779 Not all libraries restored.
CPF3780 Specified file for library not found.
CPF3783 Cannot determine VOL(*SAVVOL) location. No
         objects restored.
CPF3784 Restore device specified in the DEV parameter does
         not match VOL(*SAVVOL) device.
CPF378B Library not created.
CPF3791 End of file.
CPF3796 Storage limit exceeded for user profile.
CPF3805 Objects from save file not restored.
CPF9829 Auxiliary storage pool not found.

...

SAVLIB:
CPF3701 nn objects were saved; nn objects were not saved.
CPF3703 Object not saved.
CPF3708 Save file too small.
CPF3735 Storage limit exceeded for user profile.
CPF3749 Objects from library not saved.
CPF3751 Some libraries not saved.
CPF3771 nn objects saved. nn not saved.
CPF3777 Not all libraries saved.
CPF377E Not enough storage for save-while-active request.
CPF377F Save-while-active request prevented by pending
         record changes.
CPF3789 Only one library allowed with specified parameters.
CPF378A Message queue not available.
CPF378C SAVACTMSGQ(*WRKSTN) not valid for batch job.
CPF378E Library not saved.
CPF3790 No available space on mounted diskette.
CPF3797 No objects saved from library. Save limit exceeded.

CPF379E Not enough storage available to save library.
CPF380B Save cannot be completed at this time.
CPF3815 Save file too small for save operation.
CPF3871 No objects saved or restored; nn objects not included.
CPF3892 Object not saved.
...

SAVLICPGM (Save Licensed Program)
RSTLICPGM (Restore Licensed Program)
These commands save and restore objects that make up IBM-supplied licensed programs. SAVLICPGM saves the objects to offline media. RSTLICPGM restores the objects to the system.

Files Used
RSTLICPGM:

QSYS/QPSRLDSP	*PRTF	Restored objects printer file.

Common MONMSG Messages
(All)
CPF3728 Diskette device specified with other devices.
CPF3795 Error while processing.
CPF37A2 Licensed program not valid.
CPF3884 Licensed program option not processed.
...

RSTLICPGM:
CPF3820 nn objects for option not restored.
CPF3880 No language objects exist.
CPF3D96 Objects for product not restored.
CPI36C9 Error occurred while removing PTFs.
PFR0004 Cannot install Performance Tools Subset/400 LPO over Performance Tools/400 LPP.
...

SAVOBJ (Save Object) — See also CHKOBJ, CPROBJ, CRTDUPOBJ, DMPOBJ, MOVOBJ, RNMOBJ, WRKOBJ, WRKOBJLCK
RSTOBJ (Restore Object)
SAVCHGOBJ (Save Changed Object)
These commands save and restore objects. SAVOBJ saves one or more objects in a library to offline media, or to a save file. RSTOBJ restores the objects to the system. SAVCHGOBJ saves only those objects that have changed since a referenced date and time.

Files Used
RSTOBJ:

QSYS/QASRRSTO	*PF	Model OUTFILE for restored objects.
QSYS/QPSRLDSP	*PRTF	Restored objects printer file.

SAVCHGOBJ, SAVOBJ:

QSYS/QASAVOBJ	*PF	Model OUTFILE for saved objects.
QSYS/QPSAVOBJ	*PRTF	Save objects printer file.

Common MONMSG Messages

(All)

CPF3709	Tape devices do not support same densities.
CPF3727	Duplicate device specified in device name list.
CPF3728	Diskette device specified with other devices.
CPF3730	Not authorized to object.
CPF3731	Cannot use object.
CPF3767	Device not found.
CPF3768	Device not valid for command.
CPF3770	No objects saved or restored for library.
CPF3781	Library not found.
CPF3782	File not a save file.
CPF3793	Machine storage limit reached.
CPF3794	Save or restore operation ended unsuccessfully.
CPF3795	Error while processing.
CPF3812	Save file in use.
CPF3871	No objects saved or restored; nn objects not included.
CPF5729	Not able to allocate object.
CPF9809	Library cannot be accessed.
CPF9812	File not found.
CPF9820	Not authorized to use library.
CPF9822	Not authorized to file.
CPF9825	Not authorized to device.

...

RSTOBJ:

CPF3705	Object not journaled.
CPF3706	Object not restored to library.
CPF3707	Save file contains no data.
CPF370C	Not authorized to ALWOBJDIF parameter.
CPF3743	File cannot be restored, displayed, or listed.
CPF374C	No objects restored to ASP.
CPF3769	File found on media not save/restore file.
CPF3773	nn objects restored. nn not restored.
CPF3780	Specified file not found.
CPF3791	End of file.
CPF3796	Storage limit exceeded for user profile.
CPF3805	Objects from save file not restored.
CPF3872	Not all objects restored.
CPF9829	Auxiliary storage pool not found.

...

SAVCHGOBJ:

CPF3702	nn objects saved; nn not saved; nn not included.
CPF3703	Object not saved.
CPF3708	Save file too small.
CPF3735	Storage limit exceeded for user profile.
CPF3745	No record of SAVLIB operation exists.
CPF3746	System date and time earlier than reference date and time.
CPF3747	Object names cannot be specified with more than one library.
CPF3749	Objects not saved.

CPF3774	Not all objects saved.
CPF3778	Not all objects saved from all libraries.
CPF377E	Not enough storage for save-while-active request.
CPF377F	Save-while-active request prevented by pending record changes.
CPF3789	Only one library allowed with specified parameters.
CPF378A	Message queue not available.
CPF378C	SAVACTMSGQ(*WRKSTN) not valid for batch job.
CPF378E	Library not saved.
CPF3790	No available space on mounted diskette.
CPF3797	No objects saved from library. Save limit exceeded.
CPF379E	Not enough storage available to save library.
CPF380B	Save cannot be completed at this time.
CPF3815	Save file too small for save operation.
CPF3818	Starting library not found.
CPF3892	Object not saved.
CPF3894	Cancel reply received for message.

...

SAVOBJ:

CPF3701	nn objects were saved; nn objects were not saved.
CPF3702	nn objects saved; nn not saved; nn not included.
CPF3703	Object not saved.
CPF3708	Save file too small.
CPF3735	Storage limit exceeded for user profile.
CPF3747	Object names cannot be specified with more than one library.
CPF3749	Objects not saved.
CPF3771	nn objects saved. nn not saved.
CPF3774	Not all objects saved.
CPF3778	Not all objects saved from all libraries.
CPF377E	Not enough storage for save-while-active request.
CPF377F	Save-while-active request prevented by pending record changes.
CPF3789	Only one library allowed with specified parameters.
CPF378A	Message queue not available.
CPF378C	SAVACTMSGQ(*WRKSTN) not valid for batch job.
CPF378E	Library not saved.
CPF3790	No available space on mounted diskette.
CPF3797	No objects saved. Save limit exceeded.
CPF379E	Not enough storage available to save library.
CPF380B	Save cannot be completed at this time.
CPF3815	Save file too small for save operation.
CPF3892	Object not saved.
CPF3894	Cancel reply received for message.

...

SAVSAVFDTA (Save Save File Data)

SAVSAVFDTA saves the contents of an online save file to offline media, such as tape or diskette.

Files Used

| QSYS/QASAVOBJ | *PF | Model OUTFILE for saved objects. |
| QSYS/QPSAVOBJ | *PRTF | Save objects printer file. |

Common MONMSG Messages

CPF3707	Save file contains no data.
CPF3709	Tape devices do not support same densities.
CPF3727	Duplicate device specified in device name list.
CPF3728	Diskette device specified with other devices.
CPF3767	Device not found.
CPF3768	Device not valid for command.
CPF3782	File not a save file.
CPF3793	Machine storage limit reached.
CPF3794	Save or restore operation ended unsuccessfully.
CPF3795	Error while processing.
CPF3812	Save file in use.
CPF5729	Not able to allocate object.
CPF9812	File not found.
CPF9822	Not authorized to file.
CPF9825	Not authorized to device.

...

SAVSECDTA (Save Security Data) — *See also SAVSTG, SAVSYS*

RSTAUT (Restore Authority)

RSTUSRPRF (Restore User Profiles)

These commands save and restore security related information, such as user profiles, authorization lists, and authority holders. SAVSECDTA saves the information to offline media or to an online save file. RSTUSRPRF restores user profiles to the system. RSTAUT then restores private authorities to the user profiles.

Files Used

RSTUSRPRF:

QSYS/QASRRSTO	*PF	Model OUTFILE for restored objects.

SAVSECDTA:

QSYS/QASAVOBJ	*PF	Model OUTFILE for saved objects.
QSYS/QPSAVOBJ	*PRTF	Saved objects printer file.

Common MONMSG Messages

(All except RSTAUT)

CPF3709	Tape devices do not support same densities.
CPF3727	Duplicate device specified in device name list.
CPF3728	Diskette device specified with other devices.
CPF3767	Device not found.
CPF3768	Device not valid for command.
CPF3782	File not a save file.
CPF3793	Machine storage limit reached.
CPF3794	Save or restore operation ended unsuccessfully.
CPF3795	Error while processing.
CPF3812	Save file in use.
CPF9812	File not found.

...

RSTAUT:

CPF2206	User needs authority to do requested function on object.
CPF3776	Not all user profiles had all authorities restored.

CPF3785 Not all subsystems ended.

RSTUSRPRF:

CPD3774 USRPRF(*ALL) required when MAIL(*YES) specified.
CPF2206 User needs authority to do requested function on object.
CPF370C Not authorized to ALWOBJDIF parameter.
CPF3743 File cannot be restored, displayed, or listed.
CPF376B File not found.
CPF3775 Not all user profiles or authority objects restored.
CPF3780 Specified file for library not found.
CPF3785 Not all subsystems ended.
CPF3796 Storage limit exceeded for user profile.
CPF908A Requester not enrolled.
...

SAVSECDTA:

CPF370A Not all security objects saved to save file.
CPF3731 Cannot use object.
CPF3735 Storage limit exceeded for user profile.
CPF3737 Save and restore data area not found.
CPF3893 Not all security objects saved.
CPF3894 Cancel reply received for message.
CPF5729 Not able to allocate object.
CPF9809 Library cannot be accessed.
CPF9847 Error occurred while closing file.
CPF9850 Override of printer file not allowed.
CPF9851 Overflow value for file too small.
CPF9860 Error occurred during output file processing.

SAVSTG (Save Storage)

Saves the entire contents of the licensed internal code and all disk storage to a tape. You cannot restore individual libraries or objects from the resulting tape; you can only replace the entire system, using dedicated storage tools.

MONMSG Messages

CPF2206 User needs authority to do requested function on object.
CPF3767 Device not found.
CPF3768 Device not valid for command.
CPF376A Keylock switch not in correct position.
CPF3785 Not all subsystems ended.

SAVSYS (Save System)

Saves licensed internal code, the contents of the QSYS system library, configuration information, and security information to offline media. The tape can be used to recover the system library.

Files Used

QSYS/QASAVOBJ	*PF	Model OUTFILE for saved objects.
QSYS/QPSAVOBJ	*PRTF	Saved objects printer file.

Common MONMSG Messages

CPF2206 User needs authority to do requested function on object.
CPF3703 Object not saved.
CPF3709 Tape devices do not support same densities.

CPF3727	Duplicate device specified in device name list.
CPF3728	Diskette device specified with other devices.
CPF372B	Not all objects were saved.
CPF3735	Storage limit exceeded for user profile.
CPF3767	Device not found.
CPF3768	Device not valid for command.
CPF3772	SAVSYS completed. One or more objects not saved.
CPF3785	Not all subsystems ended.
CPF3793	Machine storage limit reached.
CPF3794	Save or restore operation ended unsuccessfully.
CPF3795	Error while processing.
CPF3797	No objects saved from library. Save limit exceeded.
CPF3798	Installation not found.
CPF3873	Licensed program not saved.
CPF3894	Cancel reply received for message.
CPF9847	Error occurred while closing file.
CPF9850	Override of printer file not allowed.
CPF9851	Overflow value for file too small.
CPF9860	Error occurred during output file processing.

...

SBMJOB (Submit Job)

Submits a job to a job queue for later processing as a batch job.

MONMSG Messages

| CPF1338 | Errors occurred on SBMJOB command. |
| CPF1651 | Sort sequence table not accessed. |

SETATNPGM (Set Attention Program)

Sets a specified program as the attention key handling program at the current invocation level. You can use this command to set the attention key handler on or off.

MONMSG Messages

| CPF1318 | Attention key program not set. |

SETOBJACC (Set Object Access)

Forces an object into or out of a main storage pool. Bringing an object into a main storage pool will speed access to that object.

MONMSG Messages

CPF1858	The specified pool does not exist.
CPF1859	Use of an access path was requested but none exists.
CPF9855	File contains no members.

SIGNOFF (Sign Off) — *See also DSCJOB*

Ends an interactive job.

MONMSG Messages

(None)

SNDBRKMSG (Send Break Message) — *See SNDMSG*
SNDF (Send File) — *See RCVF*

SNDMSG (Send Message) — *See also RCVMSG*

SNDBRKMSG (Send Break Message)
SNDPGMMSG (Send Program Message)
SNDRPY (Send Reply)
SNDUSRMSG (Send User Message)

These commands send messages to a message queue. SNDMSG sends an impromptu message to one or more message queues. SNDBRKMSG sends an impromptu message (*INFO or *INQ) to one or more workstation message queues, interrupting the workstation to display the message. SNDPGMMSG lets a CL program send a predefined or an impromptu message to a program's message queue within a job or to the job's external (*EXT) message queue. SNDUSRMSG is used by a CL program to send an impromptu or a predefined message to a message queue and optionally receive a reply, placing the reply into a CL variable. SNDRPY sends a reply to the sender of an inquiry (*INQ) message.

MONMSG Messages

(All except SNDRPY, SNDUSRMSG)

CPF2428	Only one message queue allowed for *INQ and *NOTIFY type messages.
CPF2469	Error occurred when sending message.

SNDBRKMSG:

CPF9838	User profile storage limit exceeded.

SNDMSG:

CPF2433	Function not allowed for system log message queue.
CPF2488	Reply message queue *WRKSTN not valid for batch job.
CPF9838	User profile storage limit exceeded.

SNDPGMMSG:

CPF2453	Reply queue not sender's program message queue.
CPF2479	Call stack entry not found.
CPF247A	Call stack entry not found.
CPF2499	Message identifier not allowed.
CPF2524	Exception handler not available.
CPF2550	Exception message sent to a deleted program or procedure.
CPF9847	Error occurred while closing file.

SNDRPY:

CPF2401	Not authorized to library.
CPF2403	Message queue not found.
CPF2408	Not authorized to message queue.
CPF2410	Message key not found in message queue.
CPF2411	Not authorized to message file.
CPF2420	Reply already sent for inquiry or notify message.
CPF2422	Reply not valid.
CPF2432	Cannot send reply to message type other than *INQ or *NOTIFY.
CPF2433	Function not allowed for system log message queue.
CPF2460	Message queue could not be extended.
CPF2471	Length of field not valid.
CPF2477	Message queue currently in use.
CPF9838	User profile storage limit exceeded.

...

SNDUSRMSG:

CPF2559	Error occurred in SNDUSRMSG command.

SNDPGMMSG (Send Program Message) — *See SNDMSG*
SNDRCVF (Send/Receive File) — *See RCVF*

SNDRPY (Send Reply) — *See SNDMSG*

SNDUSRMSG (Send User Message) — *See SNDUSRMSG*

STRCPYSCN (Start Copy Screen)

ENDCPYSCN (End Copy Screen)

These commands start and end the function that lets you copy a workstation screen to another station to observe the screen and diagnose problems. You can also copy a workstation screen to a database file. STRCPYSCN starts the function; ENDCPYSCN ends the function.

Note: If the OUTDEV is a workstation, and you cannot access a comand line to execute ENDCPYSCN, you can press the SYSREQ key, then enter ENDCPYSCN.

Files Used

QSYS/QASCCPY	*PF	Model OUTFILE for copy screen output.

MONMSG Messages

(All)

CPF2207   Not authorized to use object.

CPF7AF7   Device name not correct.

ENDCPYSCN:

CPF7AF8   Device name not being copied.

STRCPYSCN:

CPF7AF4   Library QTEMP is not valid for OUTFILE keyword.

CPF7AF5   From device cannot be used with to device.

CPF7AF6   Device not available.

CPF9860   Error occurred during output file processing.

CPI7AF9   Screen image not displayed.

STRDBG (Start Debug)

ADDBKP (Add Breakpoint)

ADDPGM (Add Program)

ADDTRC (Add Trace)

CHGDBG (Change Debug)

CHGPGMVAR (Change Program Variable)

CLRTRCDTA (Clear Trace Data)

DSPBKP (Display Breakpoints)

DSPDBG (Display Debug)

DSPPGMVAR (Display Program Variable)

DSPTRC (Display Trace)

DSPTRCDTA (Display Trace Data)

ENDDBG (End Debug)

RMVBKP (Remove Breakpoint)

RMVPGM (Remove Program)

RMVTRC (Remove Trace)

RSMBKP (Resume Breakpoint)

These commands manage debug mode. In debug mode, you can monitor the execution of a program, and view the contents of variables within the program. STRDBG starts debug mode, and optionally specifies one or more programs to be debugged. ENDDBG ends debug mode. CHGDBG changes some of the attributes of the debug session. DSPDBG shows the current status of the debug session.

ADDPGM adds one or more programs to the group of programs being debugged. For these programs you can specify breakpoints and traces, to help monitor their progress. RMVPGM removes one or more programs from the debug group.

ADDBKP adds one or more breakpoints to a debugged program. At a breakpoint, the program stops processing and passes control to the user. DSPBKP shows all the currently set breakpoints. RMVBKP removes a breakpoint. RSMBKP causes a program to continue after pausing at a breakpoint.

DSPPGMVAR shows the current value of a program variable at a breakpoint. CHGPGMVAR changes the value of the variable.

ADDTRC specifies one or more ranges of program statements to trace in a debug session. The system will record the sequence in which traced statements are executed. DSPTRC shows the currently specified trace ranges. RMVTRC removes one or more range of program statements from the trace group. DSPTRCDTA shows the trace information; CLRTRCDTA clears the trace information.

Files Used (by DSPxxx Commands)
QSYS/QPDBGDSP   *PRTF   Debug display printer file.

MONMSG Messages
(All except DSPDBG)
CPF1999   Errors occurred on command.

DSPDBG:
(None)

STRPRTWTR (Start Printer Writer) — *See WRKWTR*
STRSBS (Start Subsystem) — *See WRKSBS*

TFRCTL (Transfer Control)
In a CL program, TFRCTL calls a program, passes control to it, and removes the calling program from the invocation stack. The called program runs at the same invocation level as the calling program. Using TFRCTL may improve performance.

MONMSG Messages
CPF0805   Error found when program started.
CPF0809   Transfer control (TFRCTL) to C program not allowed.

TFRGRPJOB (Transfer to Group Job) — *See also CHGGRPA*
ENDGRPJOB (End Group Job)
These commands navigate among group jobs. A group job is one of up to 16 interactive jobs that are associated as a group. You can transfer control from one group job to another without ending either of the group jobs. TFRGRPJOB suspends the current job and resumes another group job, transferring control to it. ENDGRPJOB ends a group job, then resumes another job in the group.

MONMSG Messages
ENDGRPJOB:
CPF1309   Subsystem cannot complete the command.
CPF1314   Value not allowed.
CPF1317   No response from subsystem.
CPF1322   ENDGRPJOB command not allowed at this time.
CPF1323   Group job not ended; parameters do not agree.
CPF1324   Group job not ended; parameters do not agree.
CPF1325   Group job not ended; group job does not exist.
CPF1326   Group job does not exist.
CPF1327   Cannot end group job with ENDGRPJOB.

CPF1351 Function check occurred in subsystem for job.

TFRGRPJOB:
CPF1310 Request to transfer to group job failed.
CPF1313 Value not allowed name.
CPF1314 Value not allowed.
CPF1E15 Problem occurred while calling Operational Assistant.

TFRJOB (Transfer Job) — *See WRKJOB*
TFRSECJOB (Transfer Secondary Job) — *See WRKJOB*
VRYCFG (Vary Configuration) — *See WRKCFGSTS*
WAIT (Wait) — *See RCVF*
WRKACTJOB (Work with Active Jobs) — *See WRKJOB*

WRKAUTL (Work with Authorization Lists)
    ADDAUTLE (Add Authorization List Entry)
    CHGAUTLE (Change Authorization List Entry)
    CRTAUTL (Create Authorization List)
    DLTAUTL (Delete Authorization List)
    DSPAUTL (Display Authorization List)
    DSPAUTLOBJ (Display Authorization List Objects)
    EDTAUTL (Edit Authorization List)
    RMVAUTLE (Remove Authorization List Entry)
    RTVAUTLE (Retrieve Authorization List Entry)

These commands manipulate authorization lists. Authorization lists are used to grant object authority to a group of users. CRTAUTL creates a new authorization list. DSPAUTL shows the users that make up an authorization list. DSPAUTLOBJ shows objects secured by an authorization list. EDTAUTL shows the users in an authorization list, and lets you edit the entries in the list. DLTAUTL deletes an authorization list.

ADDAUTLE adds a user to an authorization list. CHGAUTLE changes an entry in an authorization list. RMVAUTLE removes an entry from an authorization list.

RTVAUTLE is used in a CL program to retrieve the contents of an authorization list entry into CL program variables. The following parameters retrieve the information:

ADD	*CHAR 10	*ADD authority.
ALL	*CHAR 10	*ALL authority.
AUTLMGT	*CHAR 10	*AUTLMGT authority.
CHANGE	*CHAR 10	*CHANGE authority.
DELETE	*CHAR 10	*DELETE authority.
EXCLUDE	*CHAR 10	*EXCLUDE authority.
OBJEXIST	*CHAR 10	*OBJEXIST authority.
OBJMGT	*CHAR 10	*OBJMGT authrity.
OBJOPR	*CHAR 10	*OBJOPR authority.
READ	*CHAR 10	*READ authority.
UPDATE	*CHAR 10	*UPDATE authority.
USE	*CHAR 10	*USE authority.

Files Used

DSPAUTL:

QSYS/QAOBJAUT	*PF	Model OUTFILE.
QSYS/QPOBJAUT	*PRTF	Authorization list entries printer file.

Common MONMSG Messages

ADDAUTLE:

CPF2253	No objects found.
CPF2280	*PUBLIC is always on authorization list, cannot be added.
CPF2281	The users specified do not exist on the system.
CPF2282	nn errors adding users, nn authorization lists processed.
CPF2283	Authorization list does not exist.
CPF2284	Not authorized to change authorization list.
CPF2289	Unable to allocate authorization list.
CPF2290	*EXCLUDE cannot be specified with another authority.
CPF22AA	Only *AUTLMGT authority can be specified with *ALL authority.
CPF22AB	Only *AUTLMGT can be specified with *CHANGE authority.
CPF22AC	Only *AUTLMGT authority can be specified with *USE authority.

CHGAUTLE:

CPF2253	No objects found.
CPF2281	The users specified do not exist on the system.
CPF2283	Authorization list does not exist.
CPF2284	Not authorized to change authorization list.
CPF2286	*PUBLIC cannot be given *AUTLMGT authority.
CPF2287	nn errors changing users, nn authorization lists processed.
CPF2289	Unable to allocate authorization list.
CPF2290	*EXCLUDE cannot be specified with another authority.
CPF22AA	Only *AUTLMGT authority can be specified with *ALL authority.
CPF22AB	Only *AUTLMGT can be specified with *CHANGE authority.
CPF22AC	Only *AUTLMGT authority can be specified with *USE authority.

CRTAUTL:

CPF2122	Storage limit exceeded for user profile.
CPF2204	User profile not found.
CPF2217	Not authorized to user profile.
CPF2222	Storage limit is greater than specified for user profile.
CPF2278	Authorization list already exists.
CPF2289	Unable to allocate authorization list.
CPF22A6	User creating an authorization list must have *ADD authority to his user profile.
CPF22AD	Group profile for user not found.

DLTAUTL:

CPF2105	Object not found.
CPF2110	Library not found.
CPF2113	Cannot allocate library.
CPF2114	Cannot allocate object.
CPF2117	nn objects deleted. nn objects not deleted.

CPF2125	No objects deleted.
CPF2160	Object type not eligible for requested function.
CPF2182	Not authorized to library.
CPF2189	Not authorized to object.
CPF2279	Authorization list cannot be deleted.
CPF2289	Unable to allocate authorization list.
CPF9801	Object not found.

...

DSPAUTL:

CPF2204	User profile not found.
CPF2207	Not authorized to use object.
CPF2208	Object not found.
CPF2209	Library not found.
CPF2211	Not able to allocate object.
CPF2216	Not authorized to use library.
CPF2283	Authorization list does not exist.
CPF9843	Object cannot be accessed.
CPF9850	Override of printer file not allowed.
CPF9851	Overflow value for file too small.
CPF9860	Error occurred during output file processing.

DSPAUTLOBJ:

CPF2283	Authorization list does not exist.
CPF2289	Unable to allocate authorization list.
CPF22AF	Not authorized to authorization list.
CPF9850	Override of printer file not allowed.
CPF9851	Overflow value for file too small.
CPF9860	Error occurred during output file processing.

EDTAUTL:

CPF2204	User profile not found.
CPF2207	Not authorized to use object.
CPF2208	Object not found.
CPF2209	Library not found.
CPF2211	Not able to allocate object.
CPF2216	Not authorized to use library.
CPF2217	Not authorized to user profile.
CPF2283	Authorization list does not exist.
CPF22B9	Not authorized to change authorities.
CPF9843	Object cannot be accessed.

RMVAUTLE:

CPF2253	No objects found.
CPF2281	The users specified do not exist on the system.
CPF2283	Authorization list does not exist.
CPF2284	Not authorized to change authorization list.
CPF2285	nn errors removing users, nn authorization lists processed.
CPF2288	*PUBLIC cannot be removed from an authorization list.
CPF2289	Unable to allocate authorization list.

RTVAUTLE:

CPF2283	Authorization list does not exist.
CPF2289	Unable to allocate authorization list.
CPF22A7	User not on authorization list, no authorities retrieved.

CPF22A8   Not authorized to retrieve authorities for user.

WRKAUTL:
(None)

WRKBNDDIR (Work with Binding Directories)
ADDBNDDIRE (Add Binding Directory Entry)
CRTBNDDIR (Create Binding Directory)
DLTBNDDIR (Delete Binding Directory)
DSPBNDDIR (Display Binding Directory)
RMVBNDDIRE (Remove Binding Directory Entry)
WRKBNDDIRE (Work with Binding Directory Entries)

These commands manage binding directories and their entries. A binding directory is a list of modules and service programs. WRKBINDIR displays a list of binding directories that you can work with. CRTBNDDIR creates a new binding directory. DLTBNDDIR deletes an existing binding directory, while DSPBNDDIR displays the contents of a binding directory.

ADDBNDDIRE adds an entry to an existing binding directory, and RMVBNDDIRE removes one. WRKBNDDIRE lets you work with the entries in a binding directory.

Files Used
DSPBNDDIR:

QSYS/QABNDBND	*PF	Model OUTFILE.
QSYS/QSYSPRT	*PRTF	Binding directory printer file.

MONMSG Messages
(All except CRTBNDDIR, DLTBNDDIR, WRKBNDDIR)
CPF5D01   Binding directory is not usable.
CPF9801   Object not found.
CPF9802   Not authorized to object.
CPF980F   Binding directory not found.
CPF9820   Not authorized to use library.

ADDBNDDIRE:
CPF5D09   Object was not found in binding directory.

CRTBNDDIR:
CPF5D0B   Binding directory was not created

DLTBNDDIR:
(None)

RMVBNDDIRE:
CPF5D09   Object was not found in binding directory.

WRKBINDIR:
CPF5D0B   Binding directory was not created
CPF980F   Binding directory not found.

WRKBNDDIRE (Work with Binding Directory Entries) — *See WRKBNDDIR*

WRKCFGSTS (Work with Configuration Status)
RTVCFGSTS (Retrieve Configuration Status)
VRYCFG (Vary Configuration)

These commands manipulate the status of configuration objects, including lines, controllers, and devices. WRKCFGSTS shows the objects, and lets you display their status or their descriptions, or vary them on or off. VRYCFG varies a line, controller, or device on or off.

RTVCFGSTS retrieves the current status of a line, controller, or devices, placing the status in a CL program variable (*DEC (5 0)), identified by the STSCDE parameter. The status codes are:

    0=Varied off
    10=Vary off pending
    20=Vary on pending
    30=Varied on
    40=Connect pending
    50=Signon display
    60=Active
    70=Held
    80=Recovery pending
    90=Recovery cancelled
    100=Failed
    110=Diagnostic mode
    111=Damaged
    112=Locked
    113=Unknown

Files Used

WRKCFGSTS:

QSYS/QSYSPRT	*PRTF	Configuration status printer file.

Common MONMSG Messages

RTVCFGSTS:

CPF9801	Object not found.
CPF9802	Not authorized to object.

VRYCFG:

CPF2640	Vary command not processed.
CPF2659	Vary command may not have completed.

...

WRKCFGSTS:

CPF1E99	Unexpected error occurred.
CPF2602	Controller not found.
CPF2702	Device description not found.
CPF2703	Controller description not found.
CPF2704	Line description not found.

WRKCMD (Work with Commands)

CHGCMD (Change Command)
CHGCMDDFT (Change Command Default)
CRTCMD (Create Command)
DLTCMD (Delete Command)
DSPCMD (Display Command)

These commands manipulate command objects. CRTCMD creates a new command, using source data in a source physical file member. CHGCMD changes certain properties of a command; CHGCMDDFT lets you change the default value of a command parameter. DSPCMD shows the attributes of a command. DLTCMD deletes a command from the system.

Files Used

CRTCMD:

QGPL/QCMDSRC	*PF	Source default input file.
QSYS/QSYSPRT	*PRTF	Source listing printer file.

DSPCMD:
QSYS/QPCMD   *PRTF   Command values printer
                                             file.

Common MONMSG Messages

CHGCMD:

CPF6209	Library not found.
CPF6210	Command not found.
CPF6211	Not authorized to change command.
CPF6212	Command not changed.
CPF6213	Cannot allocate command.
CPF6214	Errors detected while changing command.
CPF6215	Command cannot be changed.
CPF6219	Not authorized to library.

CHGCMDDFT:

CPF6260	Errors detected while changing defaults.
CPF6261	Cannot change command.

CRTCMD:

CPF0201	Command not created.
CPF0210	Cannot open printer file.
CPF0212	Unable to open source file.

DLTCMD:

CPF2105	Object not found.
CPF2110	Library not found.
CPF2113	Cannot allocate library.
CPF2114	Cannot allocate object.
CPF2117	nn objects deleted. nn objects not deleted.
CPF2182	Not authorized to library.
CPF2189	Not authorized to object.

...

DSPCMD:

CPF2150	Object information function failed.
CPF2151	Operation failed.
CPF6210	Command not found.
CPF6250	Cannot display or retrieve command.
CPF9802	Not authorized to object.
CPF9820	Not authorized to use library.
CPF9824	Not authorized to command.

...

WRKCMD:

CPF9809	Library cannot be accessed.
CPF9820	Not authorized to use library.

WRKDIR (Work with Directory)

ADDDIRE (Add Directory Entry)
CHGDIRE (Change Directory Entry)
DSPDIR (Display Directory)
RMVDIRE (Remove Directory Entry)
RNMDIRE (Rename Directory Entry)

These commands manage entries in the system distribution directory.
The directory entries contain a user identifier, profile name, address,
system name, and user information. WRKDIR provides an interactive list
display from which to add, change, or remove directory entries. DSPDIR
shows the entries in the directory.

ADDDIRE adds a directory entry. CHGDIRE changes an entry, while RVMDIRE removes an entry. RNMDIRE renames an entry, changing the user identifier and/or address.

Files Used

DSPDIR:

QSYS/QAOSDIRO	*PF	Model OUTFILE for OUTFILFMT(*TYPE1).
QSYS/QAOSDIRB	*PF	Model OUTFILE for OUTFILFMT(*TYPE2) DETAIL(*BASIC).
QSYS/QAOSDIRF	*PF	Model OUTFILE for OUTFILFMT(*TYPE2) DETAIL(*FULL).
QSYS/QAOSDIRX	*PF	Model OUTFILE for OUTFILFMT(*TYPE3) DETAIL(*FULL).
QSYS/QPDSPDDL	*PRTF	Printer file for full detail.
QSYS/QPDSPDSM	*PRTF	Printer file for basic detail.

WRKDIR:

QSYS/QPDSPDDL	*PRTF	Printer file for full detail.
QSYS/QPDSPDSM	*PRTF	Printer file for basic detail.

Common MONMSG Messages

(All except DSPDIR, RNMDIRE, RMVDIRE)

CPF9054	Description already exists.
CPF9838	User profile storage limit exceeded.
CPI898A	Given name has been truncated.

...

ADDDIRE:

CPF9009	System requires file be journaled.
CPF9082	User ID and address not added to directory.
CPF90F2	Network user ID must be unique.

...

CHGDIRE:

CPF89AE	Directory entry for network user ID not changed.
CPF907E	You can only change your own directory entry.
CPF907F	Specified parameters not allowed.
CPF9083	User ID and address not changed.
CPF90F2	Network user ID must be unique.

...

DSPDIR:

CPF2204	User profile not found.
CPF9006	User not enrolled in system distribution directory.
CPF9009	System requires file be journaled.
CPF9820	Not authorized to use library.
CPF9822	Not authorized to file.
CPF9838	User profile storage limit exceeded.
CPF9847	Error occurred while closing file.
CPF9850	Override of printer file not allowed.
CPF9851	Overflow value for file too small.
CPF9860	Error occurred during output file processing.

...

RMVDIRE:

CPF9005	System resource required to complete this request not available.
CPF9009	System requires file be journaled.
CPF9024	System cannot get correct record to finish operation.
CPF9087	Directory entry not removed.
CPF9838	User profile storage limit exceeded.

...

RNMDIRE:

CPF897F	Rename failed.
CPI90F1	Rename completed with errors.

WRKDIR:

CPD90F9	Location does not exist.
CPF9006	User not enrolled in system distribution directory.
CPF90D9	Nickname does not exist.
CPF90E6	Department does not exist.
CPZ9002	Change of distribution lists in progress.
CPZ9003	Change of user authority in progress.

...

WRKDTAARA (Work with Data Areas)

CHGDTAARA (Change Data Area)
CRTDTAARA (Create Data Area)
DLTDTAARA (Delete Data Area)
DSPDTAARA (Display Data Area)
RTVDTAARA (Retrieve Data Area)

These commands manipulate data areas. Data areas are system objects (type *DTAARA) that store unformatted information, similar to a single record file. WRKDTAARA provides an interactive list display from which you can add, change or delete data areas. CRTDTAARA creates a new data area; DLTDTAARA deletes a data area. Use CHGDTAARA to change the contents of the data area. DSPDTAARA displays the contents of the data area. RTVDTAARA retrieves the value of all or part of a data area, placing in into a CL program variable, identified by the RTNVAR parameter.

Files Used

DSPDTAARA:

QSYS/QPDSPDTA	*PRTF	Data area printer file.

Common MONMSG Messages

(All except DLTDTAARA, WRKDTAARA)

CPF1015	Data area not found.
CPF1021	Library not found.
CPF1022	No authority to library.

CHGDTAARA:

CPF1018	No authority to change data area.
CPF1019	VALUE parameter not correct.
CPF1020	VALUE parameter too long.
CPF1026	VALUE parameter must be '0' or '1'.
CPF1046	DTAARA(*GDA) not valid because job not group job.
CPF1062	Null string not valid as character value.
CPF1063	Cannot allocate data area.
CPF1067	Cannot allocate library.

CPF1072	DTAARA(*PDA) not valid because job not prestart job.
CPF1087	Substring not allowed for decimal or logical data area.
CPF1088	Starting position outside of data area.
CPF1089	Substring specified for data area not valid.
CPF1138	VALUE parameter not valid type.
CPF1155	VALUE parameter too long.
CPF1170	Starting position outside of data area.
CPF1192	Substring specified not valid.

...

CRTDTAARA:

CPF1008	Data area not created.
CPF1023	Data area exists.
CPF1024	TYPE and VALUE parameters not compatible.
CPF1025	LEN and VALUE parameters not compatible.
CPF1026	VALUE parameter must be '0' or '1'.
CPF1047	Length not valid.
CPF1062	Null string not valid as character value.
CPF1092	Cannot create data area.
CPF9802	Not authorized to object.

DLTDTAARA:

CPF2105	Object not found.
CPF2110	Library not found.
CPF2113	Cannot allocate library.
CPF2114	Cannot allocate object.
CPF2117	nn objects deleted. nn objects not deleted.
CPF2182	Not authorized to library.
CPF2189	Not authorized to object.

...

DSPDTAARA:

CPF1016	No authority to data area.
CPF1046	DTAARA(*GDA) not valid because job not group job.
CPF1063	Cannot allocate data area.
CPF1067	Cannot allocate library.
CPF1072	DTAARA(*PDA) not valid because job not prestart job.
CPF9847	Error occurred while closing file.
CPF9850	Override of printer file not allowed.
CPF9851	Overflow value for file too small.

...

RTVDTAARA:

CPF0811	RTNVAR parameter has incorrect length for data area.
CPF0812	RTNVAR parameter type not valid for data area.
CPF0813	Value in data area not logical value.
CPF1016	No authority to data area.
CPF1046	DTAARA(*GDA) not valid because job not group job.
CPF1063	Cannot allocate data area.
CPF1067	Cannot allocate library.
CPF1072	DTAARA(*PDA) not valid because job not prestart job.

	CPF1087	Substring not allowed for decimal or logical data area.
	CPF1088	Starting position outside of data area.
	CPF1089	Substring specified for data area not valid.
	...	

WRKDTAARA:
CPF9809   Library cannot be accessed.

WRKDTAQ (Work with Data Queues)
CRTDTAQ (Create Data Queue)
DLTDTAQ (Delete Data Queue)
These commands manipulate data queues. Data queues are system
objects (type *DTAQ) that act as temporary holding areas for data that is
typically sent by one program, then received by another. WRKDTAQ
provides an interactive list display from which to add or delete data
queues. CRTDTAQ creates a new data queue; DLTDTAQ deletes an
existing data queue from the system.

There are no commands to manipulate the data entries in a data
queue. To send data to a data queue, use the IBM-provided API
QSNDDTAQ; another API, QRCVDTAQ, reads entries from a data
queue.

MONMSG Messages

CRTDTAQ:
CPF2108   Object not added to library. Function check occurred.
CPF2151   Operation failed.
CPF2283   Authorization list does not exist.
CPF6565   User profile storage limit exceeded.
CPF9820   Not authorized to use library.
CPF9870   Object already exists.

DLTDTAQ:
CPF2105   Object not found.
CPF2110   Library not found.
CPF2113   Cannot allocate library.
CPF2117   nn objects deleted. nn objects not deleted.
CPF2182   Not authorized to library.
CPF2189   Not authorized to object.

WRKDTAQ:
CPF9809   Library cannot be accessed.

WRKJOB (Work with Job) — See also DSPJOBLOG, SBMJOB, SIGNOFF
CHGJOB (Change Job)
DMPJOB (Dump Job)
DSPJOB (Display Job)
ENDJOB (End Job)
ENDJOBABN (End Job Abnormal)
HLDJOB (Hold Job)
RLSJOB (Release Job)
RTVJOBA (Retrieve Job Attributes)
TFRJOB (Transfer Job)
TFRSECJOB (Transfer Secondary Job)
WRKACTJOB (Work with Active Jobs)
WRKSBMJOB (Work with Submitted Jobs)

WRKSBSJOB (Work with Subsystem Jobs)
WRKUSRJOB (Work with User Jobs)
These commands manage jobs on the system. WRKJOB shows information about a single job, and lets you change certain properties or information about the job. WRKACTJOB presents an interactive list display of active jobs, which you can use to manage the jobs, including changing, ending, or displaying them. WRKSBMJOB performs a similar function for jobs that have been submitted to a job queue; WRKUSRJOB does the same for user jobs, both interactive and batch.

CHGJOB changes a single job's attributes, such as its job queue, output queue, or priority. DMPJOB prints a report showing the contents of the basic structure of a job, and other debugging information. DSPJOB shows a job's properties, but does not let you change them.

ENDJOB ends a job, either while it is running, or while it is waiting on a job queue. If the system will not respond within ten minutes when you try to end a job with OPTION(*IMMED), ENDJOBABN will end the job abnormally.

HLDJOB holds a job, making it ineligible for processing; you can hold a job while it is running or while it is waiting on a job queue. RLSJOB releases a held job to make it eligible for processing.

TFRJOB transfers a job to a job queue, usually to allow it to run in a different subsystem than the one in which it is currently running.

TFRSECJOB allows you to create a second interactive job at a workstation, then transfer back and forth between the original (primary) job and the new (secondary) job. This command is also invoked by option 1 on the System Request menu, available by pressing SysRq.

RTVJOBA retrieves one or more attributes of a job, placing them into a CL program variable. Use the following parameters to retrieve the information:

ACGCDE	*CHAR 15	Accounting code.
BRKMSG	*CHAR 7	Break message handling mode.
CCSID	*DEC (5 0)	Coded character set identifier.
CNTRYID	*CHAR 2	Country identifier (*CHAR 2).
CURLIB	*CHAR 10	Current library for job, or *NONE.
CURUSER	*CHAR 10	User profile of the current user.
DATE	*CHAR 6	Job date (DATFMT format).
DATFMT	*CHAR 4	Date format for job.
DATSEP	*CHAR 1	Date separator character for job.
DDMCNV	*CHAR 5	Action taken for DDM conversations.
DEVRCYACN	*CHAR 13	Recovery action for workstation /O errors on an interactive job.
DFTWAIT	*DEC (7 0)	Default time that system waits for an instruction to

		be processed (1-9999999 seconds, or -1=*NOMAX).
ENDSTS	*CHAR 1	Cancellation status. 1=Controlled cancel in progress, 0=No cancel in progress.
INQMSGRPY	*CHAR 10	Inquiry message handling method.
JOB	*CHAR 10	Job name.
LANGID	*CHAR 3	Language identifier.
LOGLVL	*CHAR 1	Message logging level (0 4).
LOGSEV	*DEC (2 0)	Minimum message logging severity (00-99)
LOGTYPE	*CHAR 10	Job log message text level.
LOGCLPGM	*CHAR 10	Log CL commands in job log?
NBR	*CHAR 6	Job number.
OUTQ	*CHAR 10	Output queue used for spooled output.
OUTQLIB	*CHAR 10	Library for OUTQ.
PRTDEV	*CHAR 10	Printer device.
PRTKEYFMT	*CHAR 10	Print key format (*NONE, *PRTBDR, *PRTHDR, or *PRTALL).
PRTTXT	*CHAR 30	Print text.
PURGE	*CHAR 10	Eligible for main storage purge at end of timeslice or long wait.
RTNCDE	*DEC (5 0)	Completion status code of last program in job. 0=Normal return, 1=Returned with RPG LR on, 2=Error, 3=Halt indicator set.
RUNPTY	*DEC (2 0)	Processing priority (1-99).
SBMMSGQ	*CHAR 10	Message queue.
SBMMSGQLIB	*CHAR 10	Library for SBMMSGQ.
SRTSEQ	*CHAR 10	Name of sort sequence table, or *LANGIDUNQ, *LANGIDSHR, or *HEX.
SRTSEQLIB	*CHAR 10	Library for SRTSEQ.
STSMSG	*CHAR 7	Status message handling method.
SUBTYPE	*CHAR 1	Job environment subtype. *=No subtype, E=Evoked, T=Multiple Requester Terminal (MRT), J=Prestart, P=Print driver.
SWS	*CHAR 8	Job switch values (0 or 1).
SYSLIBL	*CHAR 165	System portion of library list (up to 15 11-character fields, blank padded).

TIMSEP	*CHAR 1	Time separator character for job.	
TIMESLICE	*DEC (7 0)	Job's timeslice (1-9999999 milliseconds).	
TSEPOOL	*CHAR 10	Value indicating whether interactive jobs move to another main storage pool at end of timeslice.	
TYPE	*CHAR 1	Job environment. 0=Batch job, 1=Interactive job.	
USER	*CHAR 10	User profile associate with the job.	
USRLIBL	*CHAR 275	User portion of library list (up to 25 11-character fields, blank padded).	

Files Used

DMPJOB:
QSYS/QPSRVDMP   *PRTF   Service dump printer file.

DSPJOB, WRKJOB:
QSYS/QPDSPJOB   *PRTF   Display job printer file.

WRKACTJOB:
QSYS/QPDSPAJB   *PRTF   Active jobs printer file.

WRKSBMJOB, WRKUSRJOB:
QSYS/QPDSPSBJ   *PRTF   Submitted jobs printer file.

WRKSBSJOB:
QSYS/QPDSPSBS   *PRTF   Subsystem jobs printer file.

Common MONMSG Messages

CHGJOB:
CPF1317   No response from subsystem for job.
CPF1321   Job not found.
CPF1332   End of duplicate job names.
CPF1334   BRKMSG(*NOTIFY) only valid for interactive jobs.
CPF1336   Errors on CHGJOB command for job.
CPF1337   Job not authorized to change parameters.
CPF1340   Job control function not performed.
CPF1341   Reader or writer not allowed as job name.
CPF1343   Job not valid job type for function.
CPF1344   Not authorized to control job.
CPF1351   Function check occurred in subsystem for job.
CPF1352   Function not done. Job in transition condition.
CPF1634   Specified date or time has passed.
CPF1635   Requested change no longer allowed.
CPF1642   Schedule date not correct.
CPF1644   Scheduled date and time not changed.
CPF1650   Both scheduled date and time must be changed.
CPF1846   CHGJOB did not complete. System value not available.
...

DMPJOB:
CPF3546   Program parameters specified were not found.
CPF3560   Job being serviced not running.

CPF3563	Overflow value for file too large.
CPF3925	Cannot open file.
CPF3935	Job being serviced ended during dump.
CPF3950	Error message received for file. Request ended.
CPF3951	File cannot be overridden.
CPF3967	Dump not started because serviced job not running.
CPF3968	Dump not started because serviced job completed running.
CPF3969	Error during close of file. Output may not be complete.

...

DSPJOB:

CPF0941	Job no longer in system.
CPF1069	End of duplicate names.
CPF1070	Job not found.
CPF1071	No authority to job.
CPF2443	Job log not displayed or listed because job has ended.
CPF3330	Necessary resource not available.
CPF3336	Job no longer in the system.
CPF9847	Error occurred while closing file.
CPF9850	Override of printer file not allowed.
CPF9851	Overflow value for file too small.

ENDJOB:

CPF1317	No response from subsystem for job.
CPF1321	Job not found.
CPF1332	End of duplicate job names.
CPF1340	Job control function not performed.
CPF1341	Reader or writer not allowed as job name.
CPF1342	Current job not allowed as job name on this command.
CPF1343	Job not valid job type for function.
CPF1344	Not authorized to control job.
CPF1351	Function check occurred in subsystem for job.
CPF1352	Function not done. Job in transition condition.
CPF1359	ENDJOBABN not allowed at this time for job.
CPF1360	Job already ending because of ENDJOBABN.
CPF1361	Job already ending with *IMMED option.
CPF1362	Job has completed.
CPF1363	Job is already ending *CNTRLD.

...

ENDJOBABN:

CPF1317	No response from subsystem for job.
CPF1321	Job not found.
CPF1332	End of duplicate job names.
CPF1340	Job control function not performed.
CPF1341	Reader or writer not allowed as job name.
CPF1342	Current job not allowed as job name on this command.
CPF1343	Job not valid job type for function.
CPF1351	Function check occurred in subsystem for job.
CPF1359	ENDJOBABN not allowed at this time for job.
CPF1360	Job already ending because of ENDJOBABN.

CPF1362   Job has completed.

HLDJOB:
CPF1317   No response from subsystem for job.
CPF1321   Job not found.
CPF1332   End of duplicate job names.
CPF1340   Job control function not performed.
CPF1341   Reader or writer not allowed as job name.
CPF1342   Current job not allowed as job name on this command.
CPF1343   Job not valid job type for function.
CPF1344   Not authorized to control job.
CPF1345   Cannot hold job.
CPF1346   Job already held.
CPF1347   Cannot hold job.
CPF1348   Job held but unable to hold its files.
CPF1350   SPLFILE(*NO) specified but Job on OUTQ.
CPF1351   Function check occurred in subsystem for job.
CPF1352   Function not done. Job in transition condition.
CPF1378   Job not held at current time.
CPF1E52   Not authorized to hold job.
CPF1E53   Job has ended and cannot be held.
CPF1E54   Job cannot be held.

RLSJOB:
CPF1317   No response from subsystem for job.
CPF1321   Job not found.
CPF1332   End of duplicate job names.
CPF1340   Job control function not performed.
CPF1341   Reader or writer not allowed as job name.
CPF1343   Job not valid job type for function.
CPF1344   Not authorized to control job.
CPF1349   Job not released, the job is not held.
CPF1351   Function check occurred in subsystem for job.
CPF1352   Function not done. Job in transition condition.

RTVJOBA:
(None)

TFRJOB:
CPF1289   Transfer job is not allowed.
CPF1315   Command not allowed in this environment.
CPF1357   Job not transferred.
CPF1364   Job not transferred. Job queue not active.
CPF1365   Job not transferred. Subsystem ending.
CPF1366   Subsystem has no usable work station entry.
CPF1367   User not authorized to subsystem
CPF1368   Not authorized to job queue.
CPF1369   Job queue not found.
CPF1370   Job queue not accessible.
CPF1372   Job not transferred. Job currently being ended.
CPF1373   Job not transferred. System request in effect for job.
CPF1375   Job not transferred. Single active device not allowed to transfer.

TFRSECJOB:
CPF1380   Transfer to secondary interactive job not valid.
CPF1381   Transfer to secondary interactive job not valid.

| CPF1383 | Transfer to secondary interactive job not valid. |
| CPF1384 | Transfer to secondary interactive job not valid. |

WRKACTJOB:

CPF1093	Override of file device type not valid.
CPF9847	Error occurred while closing file.
CPF9850	Override of printer file not allowed.
CPF9851	Overflow value for file too small.

WRKJOB:

CPF0941	Job no longer in system.
CPF1069	End of duplicate names.
CPF1070	Job not found.
CPF1071	No authority to job.
CPF2443	Job log not displayed or listed because job has ended.
CPF3330	Necessary resource not available.
CPF3336	Job no longer in the system.
CPF9847	Error occurred while closing file.
CPF9850	Override of printer file not allowed.
CPF9851	Overflow value for file too small.

WRKSBMJOB:

CPF9847	Error occurred while closing file.
CPF9850	Override of printer file not allowed.
CPF9851	Overflow value for file too small.

WRKSBSJOB:

CPF1003	Subsystem not active.
CPF9847	Error occurred while closing file.
CPF9850	Override of printer file not allowed.
CPF9851	Overflow value for file too small.

WRKUSRJOB:

CPF1003	Subsystem not active.
CPF1E50	Not all jobs displayed.
CPF1E51	Job queue not found.
CPF1E99	Unexpected error occurred.
CPF9847	Error occurred while closing file.
CPF9850	Override of printer file not allowed.
CPF9851	Overflow value for file too small.

WRKJOBD (Work with Job Descriptions)

CHGJOBD (Change Job Description)
CRTJOBD (Create Job Description)
DLTJOBD (Delete Job Description)
DSPJOBD (Display Job Description)

These commands manage job descriptions. A job description is an object (type *JOBD) that describes how a job is run. WRKJOBD lets you use an interactive list display to create, change, delete, or display job descriptions. CRTJOBD creates a new job description; CHGJOBD changes some of the properties of an existing job description. DSPJOBD displays a job description's attributes, and DLTJOBD deletes a job description from the system.

Files Used

DSPJOBD:

| QSYS/QPRTJOBD | *PRTF | Job description printer file. |

Common MONMSG Messages

CHGJOBD:
CPF1625   Job description not changed.
...
CRTJOBD:
CPF1621   Job description not created.

DLTJOBD:
CPF2105   Object not found.
CPF2110   Library not found.
CPF2114   Cannot allocate object.
CPF2117   nn objects deleted. nn objects not deleted.
CPF2182   Not authorized to library.
CPF2189   Not authorized to object.

DSPJOBD:
CPF1623   Job description not displayed.
CPF9847   Error occurred while closing file.
CPF9850   Override of printer file not allowed.
CPF9851   Overflow value for file too small.
...
WRKJOBD:
CPF9809   Library cannot be accessed.

WRKJOBQ (Work with Job Queue) — *See also SBMJOB, WRKSBSD*

CLRJOBQ (Clear Job Queue)
CRTJOBQ (Create Job Queue)
DLTJOBQ (Delete Job Queue)
HLDJOBQ (Hold Job Queue)
RLSJOBQ (Release Job Queue)

These commands manage job queues. A job queue is a list of jobs waiting to be processed. It contains an entry for each waiting job. The SBMJOB (Submit Job) command is most often used to put jobs onto a job queue.

WRKJOBQ lets you manage the jobs on a job queue, using an interactive list display. CRTJOBQ creates a new job queue; DLTJOBQ deletes one from the system. HLDJOBQ holds a job queue, preventing the processing of any jobs waiting on the job queue. RLSJOBQ releases the job queue, making the waiting jobs available for processing. CLRJOBQ clears a job queue, removing all waiting jobs from the queue.

Files Used

WRKJOBQ:
QSYS/QPRTSPLQ   *PRTF   Job queue printer file.

Common MONMSG Messages

(All except CRTJOBQ, DLTJOBQ)
CPF2207   Not authorized to use object.
CPF3307   Job queue not found.
CPF3330   Necessary resource not available.

CLRJOBQ:
CPF9843   Object cannot be accessed.

CRTJOBQ:
CPF2182   Not authorized to library.
CPF2192   Object cannot be created.

CPF2207	Not authorized to use object.
CPF3323	Job queue already exists.
CPF3351	Temporary library invalid for job queue.
CPF3354	Library not found.
CPF3356	Cannot allocate library.
CPF9818	Object not created.

...

DLTJOBQ:

CPF1763	Cannot allocate one or more libraries.
CPF2105	Object not found.
CPF2110	Library not found.
CPF2117	nn objects deleted. nn objects not deleted.
CPF2182	Not authorized to library.
CPF2207	Not authorized to use object.
CPF3324	Job queue not deleted. Job queue in use.
CPF3330	Necessary resource not available.

HLDJOBQ:

| CPF3425 | Job queue already held. |

RLSJOBQ:

| CPF3423 | Job queue not released. Job queue not held. |

WRKJOBQ:

| CPF3302 | Override of print file not valid. |

WRKJOBSCDE (Work with Job Schedule Entries) — *See also* *WRKJOBQ*

ADDJOBSCDE (Add Job Schedule Entry)
CHGJOBSCDE (Change Job Schedule Entry)
HLDJOBSCDE (Hold Job Schedule Entry)
RLSJOBSCDE (Release Job Schedule Entry)
RMVJOBSCDE (Remove Job Schedule Entry)

These commands manage the system's job scheduling function. The job scheduler consists of a number of schedule entries, similar to a job queue, except the jobs are scheduled to be run on specific dates or times. The schedule entry describes a job, which the scheduler will place on a job queue on the designated date and at the designated time. The system can then process the job.

WRKJOBSCDE lets you manage the entries on the list of scheduled jobs, using an interactive list display. ADDJOBSCDE adds a new entry to the scheduler. Use CHGJOBSCDE to change an existing entry. RMVJOBSCDE removes an entry from the list. HLDJOBSCDE will prevent the scheduler from placing an entry's job on the job queue, while RLSJOBSCDE will release the entry again.

Files Used

WRKJOBSCDE:

| QSYS/QSYSPRT | *PRTF | Job schedule entries printer file. |

Common MONMSG Messages

(All except ADDJOBSCDE, CHGJOBSCDE)

CPF1628	Job schedule entry not found.
CPF1629	Not authorized to job schedule.
CPF1630	Not authorized to job schedule entry.
CPF1637	Job schedule in use.
CPF1638	Job schedule entry in use.

CPF1640   Job schedule does not exist.
...

ADDJOBSCDE:
CPF1633   Job schedule entry not added.

CHGJOBSCDE:
CPF1620   Job schedule entry not changed.

HLDJOBSCDE:
CPF1636   More than one entry with specified entry job name
           found.
CPF1645   No job schedule entries found for specified name.
CPF1646   Entry number must be *ALL when generic name
           specified.
CPF1647   nn entries successfully held, nn entries not held.
CPF1649   Entry number must be *ALL.
...

RLSJOBSCDE:
CPF1636   More than one entry with specified entry job name
           found.
CPF1645   No job schedule entries found for specified name.
CPF1646   Entry number must be *ALL when generic name
           specified.
CPF1648   nn entries successfully released. nn entries not
           released.
CPF1649   Entry number must be *ALL.
...

RMVJOBSCDE:
CPF1631   nn entries successfully removed, nn entries not
           removed.
CPF1636   More than one entry with specified entry job name
           found.
CPF1645   No job schedule entries found for specified name.
CPF1646   Entry number must be *ALL when generic name
           specified.

WRKJOBSCDE:
...

WRKLIB (Work with Libraries) — *See also CHGLIBL, SAVLIB*
    CLRLIB (Clear Library)
    CPYLIB (Copy Library)
    CRTLIB (Create Library)
    DLTLIB (Delete Library)
    DSPLIB (Display Library)
    DSPLIBD (Display Library Description)
    RTVLIBD (Retrieve Library Description)
    These commands manage libraries. A library is a "container" (i.e., an
    object that is used to hold other objects). WRKLIB lets you perform
    actions upon libraries, using an interactive list display. CRTLIB creates a
    new library. CLRLIB clears the contents of a library, without deleting
    the library; i.e., it removes the objects in the library, but keeps the
    "container." DLTLIB deletes an existing library. DSPLIB shows the
    contents of a library (i.e., the objects in the library), either displaying the
    list, printing it, or copying it to a database file. CPYLIB copies the
    contents of a library to another library.

DSPLIBD displays the description (not the contents) of a library. RTVLIBLD retrieves the description of a library, placing the information into variables in a CL program. Use the following parameters to retrieve the information:

ASP	*DEC (2 0)	Auxiliary storage pool: 1-16.
CRTAUT	*CHAR 10	Create authority value: *SYSVAL, *CHANGE, *ALL, *USE.
CRTOBJAUD	*CHAR 10	Library auditing value: *SYSVAL, *NONE, USRPRF, *CHANGE, *ALL.
TEXT	*CHAR 50	Library text description.
TYPE	*CHAR 10	Library type: PROD, TEST.

Files Used

DSPLIB:

QSYS/QPDSPLIB	*PRTF	Library printer file.

DSPLIBD:

QSYS/QPRTLIBD	*PRTF	Library description printer file.

Common MONMSG Messages

CLRLIB:

CPF2110 Library not found.
CPF2113 Cannot allocate library.
CPF2161 Cannot delete some objects in library.
CPF2182 Not authorized to library.
...

CPYLIB:

CPF2358 Library not copied or partially copied.
CPF2365 FROMLIB and TOLIB parameters cannot specify the same library.

CRTLIB:

CPF2111 Library already exists.
CPF2122 Storage limit exceeded for user profile.
CPF2138 Creation of library not allowed.
CPF2197 Library cannot be created into user ASP.
CPF2283 Authorization list does not exist.
CPF7012 Auxiliary storage pool not found for object.
CPF8D05 Library already exists.
...

DLTLIB:

CPF2110 Library not found.
CPF2113 Cannot allocate library.
CPF2161 Cannot delete some objects in library.
CPF2167 Library on library list and cannot be deleted.
CPF2168 Library not deleted.
CPF2182 Not authorized to library.
...

DSPLIB:

CPF2110   Library not found.
CPF2113   Cannot allocate library.
CPF2150   Object information function failed.
CPF2179   Cannot display library.
CPF2182   Not authorized to library.
CPF9847   Error occurred while closing file.

...

DSPLIBD:
(None)

RTVLIBD:
(None)

WRKLIB:

CPF9809   Library cannot be accessed.
CPF9820   Not authorized to use library.

WRKMNU (Work with Menus)

CHGMNU (Change Menu)
CRTMNU (Create Menu)
DLTMNU (Delete Menu)
DSPMNUA (Display Menu Attributes)

These commands manage menus. WRKMNU offers an interactive list display, from which you can create, change, and delete menus. CRTMNU creates a new menu object, CHGMNU changes the properties of an existing menu, and DLTMNU removes a menu object from the system. DSPMNUA shows the attributes of a menu.

The system suppoorts three types of menus. *DSPF menus are created from a display file and a message file. *PGM menus call a program. *UIM menus are created using source statements in a source file; the source statements conform to the rules for User Interface Manager (UIM) tag specifications.

Files Used

CRTMNU:

QGPL/QMNUSRC	*PF	Source default input file.
QSYS/QSYSPRT	*PRTF	Source listing printer file.

DSPMNUA:

QSYS/QPDSPMNU	*PRTF	Menu attributes printer file.

Common MONMSG Messages

CHGMNU:

CPF6AC2   Menu not changed.
CPF6ACD   Menu is wrong version for system.

CRTMNU:

CPF6AC3   Menu not created.

DLTMNU:

CPF2105   Object not found.
CPF2107   Library not cleared or deleted. Function check occurred.
CPF2110   Library not found.
CPF2113   Cannot allocate library.
CPF2114   Cannot allocate object.

CPF2117	nn objects deleted. nn objects not deleted.
CPF2125	No objects deleted.
CPF2160	Object type not eligible for requested function.
CPF2182	Not authorized to library.
CPF2189	Not authorized to object.

...

DSPMNUA:

CPF6ACD	Menu is wrong version for system.
CPF9801	Object not found.
CPF9802	Not authorized to object.
CPF9811	Program not found.
CPF9812	File not found.
CPF9814	Device not found.
CPF9820	Not authorized to use library.
CPF9821	Not authorized to program.
CPF9822	Not authorized to file.
CPF9825	Not authorized to device.
CPF9847	Error occurred while closing file.

...

WRKMNU:

CPF9809	Library cannot be accessed.

WRKMOD (Work with Modules)

CHGMOD (Change Module)
DLTMOD (Delete Module)
DSPMOD (Display Module)

These commands manage modules. In the Integrated Language Environment (ILE), a module is a nonexecutable object that you create using a high-level language ILE compiler, such as ILE C/400. To run a module, you must bind it into a program. WRKMOD lets you manage modules using an interactive list. CHGMOD changes certain properties of the module, without recompiling it. For example, you can use this command to optimize a module, removing redundant instructions. DLTMOD deletes a module from the system, and DSPMOD displays certain attributes of a module.

Files Used

DSPMOD:

QSYS/QABNDMBA	*PF	Model OUTFILE for basic and compatibility information.
QSYS/QABNDMSI	*PF	Model OUTFILE for decompressed size and size limits.
QSYS/QABNDMEX	*PF	Model OUTFILE for exported symbols.
QSYS/QABNDMIM	*PF	Model OUTFILE for imported symbols.
QSYS/QABNDMPR	*PF	Model OUTFILE for procedure list.

QSYS/QABNDMRE	*PF	Model OUTFILE for object references.
QSYS/QABNDMCO	*PF	Model OUTFILE for copyright information.
QSYS/QSYSPRT	*PRTF	Module printer file.

MONMSG Messages

CHGMOD:

CPF5CF7	*USRLIBL or *LIBL not allowed with a generic module name or *ALL.
CPF5CF8	Module not changed.
CPF5CF9	Module not changed.
CPF5CFA	Modules in library QSYS cannot be changed.
CPF5CFB	No modules changed.
CPF5CFC	nn changed. nn did not require change. nn not changed.
CPF5CFE	Module not changed.
CPF5CFF	Module not changed.

DLTMOD:
(None)

DSPMOD:

CPF5CE7	Error occurred while retrieving *MODULE data.
CPF9801	Object not found.
CPF9802	Not authorized to object.
CPF9820	Not authorized to use library.

WRKMOD:
(None)

WRKMSGD (Work with Message Descriptions) — *See WRKMSGF*

WRKMSGF (Work with Message Files)

ADDMSGD (Add Message Description)
CHGMSGD (Change Message Description)
CRTMSGF (Create Message File)
DLTMSGF (Delete Message File)
DSPMSGD (Display Message Descriptions)
RMVMSGD (Remove Message Description)
RTVMSG (Retrieve Message)
WRKMSGD (Work with Message Descriptions)

These commands manage message files. A message file is a special type of file that contains only predefined message descriptions. WRKMSGF lets you work with message files, using an interactive list display. CRTMSGF creates a new message file. DLTMSGF deletes a message file from the system.

WRKMSGD uses an interactive list display to let you add, change, and delete message descriptions in a message file. ADDMSGD adds a description for a new predefined message. CHGMSGD changes a message. DSPMSGD shows the details of a message description. RMVMSGD removes a predefined message from a message file.

RTVMSG retrieves a predefined message from a message file, and copies it into variables in a CL program. Use the following parameters to retrieve the information:

MSG	*CHAR 132	First level message text.
MSGLEN	*DEC (5 0)	MSG length.

SECLVL	*CHAR 3000	Second level message text.
SECLVLLEN	*DEC (5 0)	SECLVL length.
SEV	*DEC (2 0)	Message severity: 00-99.
ALROPT	*CHAR 9	Alert option.
LOGPRB	*CHAR 1	Loggable to service activity log: Y, N.

Files Used

DSPMSGD, WRKMSGD:

QSYS/QPMSGD	*PRTF	Message description printer file.

Common MONMSG Messages

(All except CRTMSGF, DLTMSGF, WRKMSGF)

CPF2401	Not authorized to library.
CPF2407	Message file not found.
CPF2411	Not authorized to message file.

ADDMSGD:

CPF2412	Message ID already exists in message file.
CPF2430	Message description not added to message file
CPF2461	Message file could not be extended.
CPF2483	Message file currently in use.
CPF9838	User profile storage limit exceeded.

...

CHGMSGD:

CPF2419	Message identifier not found in message file.
CPF2461	Message file could not be extended.
CPF2483	Message file currently in use.
CPF2499	Message identifier not allowed.
CPF2542	Message description not changed.
CPF9838	User profile storage limit exceeded.

...

CRTMSGF:

CPF2108	Object not added to library. Function check occurred.
CPF2112	Object already exists.
CPF2113	Cannot allocate library.
CPF2151	Operation failed.
CPF2182	Not authorized to library.
CPF2283	Authorization list does not exist.
CPF2402	Library not found
CPF2497	Size exceeds machine limit.
CPF9838	User profile storage limit exceeded.

DLTMSGF:

CPF2105	Object not found.
CPF2110	Library not found.
CPF2113	Cannot allocate library.
CPF2114	Cannot allocate object.
CPF2117	nn objects deleted. nn objects not deleted.
CPF2182	Not authorized to library.
CPF2189	Not authorized to object.

DSPMSGD:

CPF2483	Message file currently in use.
CPF2515	Invalid message ID range.

CPF2516   Unable to open display file.
CPF2519   Error occurred while processing message ID list.
CPF2537   Too many records written.
...

RMVMSGD:
CPF2419   Message identifier not found in message file.
CPF2483   Message file currently in use.
CPF2499   Message identifier not allowed.

RTVMSG:
CPF2419   Message identifier not found in message file.
CPF2465   Replacement text not valid for format specified.
CPF2471   Length of field not valid.
CPF2499   Message identifier not allowed.
...

WRKMSGD:
CPF2483   Message file currently in use.
CPF2499   Message identifier not allowed.
CPF2516   Unable to open display file.
...

WRKMSGF:
CPF9809   Library cannot be accessed.

WRKMSGQ (Work with Message Queues)

CHGMSGQ (Change Message Queue)
CLRMSGQ (Clear Message Queue)
CRTMSGQ (Create Message Queue)
DLTMSGQ (Delete Message Queue)

These commands deal with message queues. A message queue is an object to which the system, users, and programs can send messages, sort of an electronic "in basket." WRKMSGQ uses an interactive list display to let you manage and display message queues. CRTMSGQ creates a user-defined message queue. DLTMSGQ deletes a message queue, along with all its messages. CLRMSGQ removes the messages from a message queue, without deleting the queue itself. CHGMSGQ changes the attributes of an existing message queue.

Common MONMSG Messages

CHGMSGQ:
CPF2401   Not authorized to library.
CPF2403   Message queue not found.
CPF2406   Not authorized to break program.
CPF2408   Not authorized to message queue.
CPF2437   MSGQ(*WRKSTN) not allowed unless done interactively.
CPF2446   Delivery mode specified not valid for system log message queue.
CPF2450   Work station message queue not allocated to job.
CPF2451   Message queue is allocated to another job.
CPF2477   Message queue currently in use.
CPF2485   Number of parameters for break program message queue not valid.
CPF2507   MODE(*NOTIFY) not allowed in batch mode.
CPF2534   MSGQ(*USRPRF) specified and no msg queue with user profile.

CPF36F7 Message queue QSYSOPR is allocated to another job.

...

CLRMSGQ:
CPF2357 Message queue not cleared.

CRTMSGQ:
CPF2108 Object not added to library. Function check occurred.
CPF2112 Object already exists.
CPF2113 Cannot allocate library.
CPF2151 Operation failed.
CPF2182 Not authorized to library.
CPF2283 Authorization list does not exist.
CPF2402 Library not found
CPF2497 Size exceeds machine limit.
CPF9838 User profile storage limit exceeded.

DLTMSGQ:
CPF2105 Object not found.
CPF2110 Library not found.
CPF2117 nn objects deleted. nn objects not deleted.
CPF2182 Not authorized to library.
CPF2403 Message queue not found.
CPF2408 Not authorized to message queue.
CPF2451 Message queue is allocated to another job.
CPF2477 Message queue currently in use.
CPF2505 Deleting work station message queue not allowed.
CPF36F7 Message queue QSYSOPR is allocated to another job.

WRKMSGQ:
CPF9809 Library cannot be accessed.

WRKOBJ (Work with Objects) — *See also CHKOBJ, CPROBJ, CRTDUPOBJ, DMPOBJ, MOVOBJ, RNMOBJ, SAVOBJ, WRKOBJL*
CKCHGOBJD (Change Object Description)
DSPOBJD (Display Object Description)
RTVOBJD (Retrieve Object Description)

These commands deal with objects and object descriptions. WRKOBJ lets you manage objects (changing, deleting, displaying, etc.), using an interactive list display. CHGOBJD changes certain properties of one or more objects. DSPOBJD shows the description of one or more objects on a display, in a report, or in a database file.

RTVOBJD is used by a CL program to retrieve information from an object description, placing the information into program variables. Use the following parameters to retrieve the information:

ALWAPICHG	*CHAR 1	Allow change by program flag. '0'=Cannot change with QLICOBJD (Change Object Description) API, '1'=Change allowed with QLICOBJD.
APAR	*CHAR 10	APAR (Problem report) ID that caused this object to be patched.

APICHG	*CHAR 1	Object changed by QLICOBJD. '0'=Not changed, '1'=Changed.
ASP	*DEC (2 0)	Auxiliary storage pool ID: 1-16.
CHGDATE	*CHAR 13	Last change date: CYYMMDDHHMMSS.
COMPILER	*CHAR 16	Compiler identifier and level at creation: 5738xxxVxxRxxMxx.
CPR	*CHAR 1	Compression status. Y=Compressed, N=Not compressed, T=Temporarily decompressed, F=Saved with STG(*FREE), X=Ineligible for compression.
CRTDATE	*CHAR 13	Object creation date: CYYMMDDHHMMSS.
CRTSYSTEM	*CHAR 8	Name of the system on which the object was created.
CRTUSER	*CHAR 10	User profile of the user who created the object.
LICPGM	*CHAR 16	Licensed program identifier: 5738xxxVxxRxxMxx.
OBJATR	*CHAR 10	Extended attribute.
OBJAUD	*CHAR 10	Auditing value: *NONE, *USRPRF, *CHANGE, *ALL.
OBJDMN	*CHAR 2	Object domain. *U=User, *S=System.
OBJLVL	*CHAR 8	Object control level.
OVFASP	*CHAR 1	Object overflowed ASP flag. 0=Object did not overflow, 1=Object overflowed ASP.
OWNER	*CHAR 10	User profile of the owner.
PTF	*CHAR 10	Program Temporary Fix number.
RESETDATE	*CHAR 7	Date USEDATE last updated: CYYMMDD.
RSTDATE	*CHAR 13	Last restore date: CYYMMDDHHMMSS.
RTNLIB	*CHAR 10	Name of the library that contains the object.
SAVACTDATE	*CHAR 13	Last save-while-active date: CYYMMDDHHMMSS.
SAVCMD	*CHAR 10	Last save command used.
SAVDATE	*CHAR 13	Last save date: CYYMMDDHHMMSS.

SAVDEV	*CHAR 10		Last save device type: *SAVF, *DKT, *TAP.
SAVF	*CHAR 10		Last save file.
SAVFLIB	*CHAR 10		SAVF library.
SAVLABEL	*CHAR 17		File label of last save.
SAVSEQNBR	*DEC (4 0)		Last save tape sequence number.
SAVSIZE	*DEC (15 0)		Object size when last saved (bytes).
SAVVOL	*CHAR 71		Last save tape or diskette volume(s).
SIZE	*DEC (15 0)		Object size (bytes).
SRCDATE	*CHAR 13		Source date: CYYMMDDHHMMSS.
SRCF	*CHAR 10		Source file.
SRCFLIB	*CHAR 10		SRCF library.
SRCMBR	*CHAR 10		Source member.
STG	*CHAR 10		Storage status: *FREE, *KEEP.
SYSLVL	*CHAR 9		Operating system level at creation: VxxRxxMxx.
TEXT	*CHAR 50		Descriptive text.
USECOUNT	*DEC (5 0)		Number of days used.
USEDATE	*CHAR 7		Date of last use: CYYMMDD.
USEUPD	*CHAR 1		Log object usage: Y, N.
USRCHG	*CHAR 1		Program modified by user flag: 0=Not modified, 1=Modified by user.
USRDFNATR	*CHAR 10		User-defined attribute.

Files Used

QSYS/QADSPOBJ		*PF	Model OUTFILE for object descriptions.
QSYS/QPRTOBJD		*PRTF	Object description printer file.

Common MONMSG Messages

(All except RTVOBJD, WRKOBJ)

CPF2105	Object not found.
CPF2110	Library not found.
CPF2113	Cannot allocate library.
CPF2114	Cannot allocate object.
CPF2123	No objects of specified name or type exist in library.
CPF2150	Object information function failed.
CPF2182	Not authorized to library.
CPF2189	Not authorized to object.

...

CHGOBJD:

CPF2151	Operation failed.
CPF2198	Days used count field not reset to 0 for some objects.
CPF2451	Message queue is allocated to another job.
CPF36F7	Message queue QSYSOPR is allocated to another job.

CPF7304 File not changed.
...

DSPOBJD:
CPF2121 One or more libraries cannot be accessed.
CPF2124 No specified objects can be displayed from library.
CPF9827 Object cannot be created in library.
CPF9847 Error occurred while closing file.
CPF9850 Override of printer file not allowed.
CPF9851 Overflow value for file too small.
CPF9860 Error occurred during output file processing.
...

RTVOBJD:
CPF2150 Object information function failed.
CPF2151 Operation failed.
CPF2451 Message queue is allocated to another job.
CPF36F7 Message queue QSYSOPR is allocated to another job.
CPF9801 Object not found.
CPF9802 Not authorized to object.
CPF9811 Program not found.
CPF9812 File not found.
CPF9814 Device not found.
CPF9820 Not authorized to use library.
CPF9821 Not authorized to program.
CPF9822 Not authorized to file.
CPF9825 Not authorized to device.
...

WRKOBJ:
CPF9809 Library cannot be accessed.
CPF9820 Not authorized to use library.

WRKOBJLCK (Work with Object Locks)
ALCOBJ (Allocate Object)
CHKRCDLCK (Check Record Locks)
DLCOBJ (Deallocate Object)
DSPRCDLCK (Display Record Locks)
These commands relate to object allocation and object locking.
WRKOBJLCK lets you display and manage object lock requests, using an interactive list display.

CHKRCDLCK detects whether or not a job currently holds any record locks, sending an escape message if there are any record locks. DSPRCDLCK shows the current record lock status of one or all records in a database file member.

ALCOBJ explicitly allocates one or more objects for later use in a job. DLCOBJ explicitly deallocates the object(s).

Files Used
DSPRCDLCK:
QSYS/QPDSPRLK   *PRTF   Record locks printer file.

WRKOBJLCK:
QSYS/QPDSPOLK   *PRTF   Object locks printer file.

Common MONMSG Messages
ALCOBJ:
CPF1002 Cannot allocate objects.

CPF1040   Maximum number of objects allocated on system.
CPF1085   Objects not allocated.

CHKRCDLCK:
CPF321F   Job holds record locks.

DLCOBJ:
CPF1005   Objects not deallocated.

DSPRCDLCK:
CPF3130   Member already in use.
CPF3210   File not correct type.
CPF3247   Record does not exist in member.
CPF3275   Member not found.
CPF9812   File not found.
CPF9847   Error occurred while closing file.

WRKOBJLCK:
CPF0924   Cannot use library in library list.
CPF0935   Cannot use member name for object type.
CPF0939   Object was not found in library.
CPF0948   Member not found.
CPF0950   Object not found.
CPF0952   Library not found.
CPF0953   Library in library list previously deleted.
CPF0958   Object saved with storage freed.
CPF1093   Override of file device type not valid.
CPF9847   Error occurred while closing file.
CPF9850   Override of printer file not allowed.
CPF9851   Overflow value for file too small.
...

WRKOBJOWN (Work with Objects by Owner)
CHGOBJOWN (Change Object Owner)
These commands manage object ownership. WRKOBJOWN lets you work with objects owned by any user profile, using an interactive list display. You can edit the object authority, delete the object, display the object auhority or description, or change the object's ownership. CHGOBJOWN changes the owner of an object from one user profile to another.

Common MONMSG Messages
CHGOBJOWN:
CPF0601   Not allowed to do operation to file.
CPF0605   Device file saved with storage freed.
CPF0608   Specified user profile not available.
CPF0609   Not allowed to use specified user profile.
CPF0610   File not available.
CPF2204   User profile not found.
CPF2207   Not authorized to use object.
CPF2208   Object not found.
CPF2209   Library not found.
CPF2210   Operation not allowed for object type.
CPF2211   Not able to allocate object.
CPF2213   Not able to allocate user profile.
CPF2216   Not authorized to use library.
CPF2217   Not authorized to user profile.

CPF2222	Storage limit is greater than specified for user profile.
CPF2226	Function not done for user profile.
CPF2230	Not authorized to object.
CPF2231	Not authorized to change ownership for program.
CPF2232	Not authorized to user profile.
CPF2233	No delete authority to user profile.
CPF2298	Authority not revoked for object from user.
CPF22BD	Ownership may not have been changed for object.
CPF22BE	Function not done for user profile.
CPF3202	File in use.
CPF3203	Cannot allocate object for file.
CPF324F	File does not exist.
CPF326A	Operation not successful for file.

...

WRKOBJOWN:

CPF2204	User profile not found.
CPF2213	Not able to allocate user profile.
CPF2217	Not authorized to user profile.

WRKOUTQ (Work with Output Queue)

CHGOUTQ (Change Output Queue)
CLROUTQ (Clear Output Queue)
CRTOUTQ (Create Output Queue)
DLTOUTQ (Delete Output Queue)
HLDOUTQ (Hold Output Queue)
RLSOUTQ (Release Output Queue)
WRKOUTQD (Work with Output Queue Description)

These commands manage output queues. An output queue is a "holding area" used to store spooled files, usually reports waiting to be printed. WRKOUTQ offers an interactive list panel from which you can work with one or more output queues, or the spooled files on an output queue. CRTOUTQ creates a new output queue.

CHGOUTQ changes the attributes of an output queue. CLROUTQ removes all the entries from an output queue, without deleting the queue; DLTOUTQ deletes an existing output queue. HLDOUTQ holds an output queue, preventing the entries on the queue from being printed; RLSOUTQ releases the queue, allowing the entries to be printed.

WRKOUTQD lets you change the description of the output queue, using an interactive list display.

Files Used

WRKOUTQ:

| QSYS/QPRTSPLQ | *PRTF | Output queue printer file. |

WRKOUTQD:

| QSYS/QPDSPSQD | *PRTF | Output queue description printer file. |

Common MONMSG Messages

(All except CRTOUTQ, DLTOUTQ)

CPF2207	Not authorized to use object.
CPF3330	Necessary resource not available.
CPF3357	Output queue not found.

CHGOUTQ:

CPF3319   Cannot change number of separators. Output queue
          is active.
CPF3361   Output queue not changed. Output queue in use.
CPF33F1   Data queue not found.

CLROUTQ:

CPF9843   Object cannot be accessed.

CRTOUTQ:

CPF2182   Not authorized to library.
CPF2192   Object cannot be created.
CPF2207   Not authorized to use object.
CPF3352   Temporary library invalid for output queue.
CPF3353   Output queue already exists.
CPF3354   Library not found.
CPF3356   Cannot allocate library.
CPF33F1   Data queue not found.
CPF9818   Object not created.
...

DLTOUTQ:

CPF1763   Cannot allocate one or more libraries.
CPF2105   Object not found.
CPF2110   Library not found.
CPF2117   nn objects deleted. nn objects not deleted.
CPF2182   Not authorized to library.
CPF2207   Not authorized to use object.
CPF3330   Necessary resource not available.
CPF3360   Output queue not deleted. Output queue in use.
CPF3467   Output queue deleted and then created again.
CPF3469   Operation not allowed for output queue.

HLDOUTQ:

CPF3426   Output queue already held.

RLSOUTQ:

CPF3424   Output queue not released. Output queue not held.

WRKOUTQ:

CPF3302   Override of print file not valid.

WRKOUTQD:

CPF2150   Object information function failed.
CPF2151   Operation failed.
CPF3302   Override of print file not valid.

WRKOUTQD (Work with Output Queue Description) — *See*
WRKOUTQ

WRKPGM (Work with Programs) — *See also CRTCLPGM*

CHGPGM (Change Program)
CRTPGM (Create Program)
DLTPGM (Delete Program)
DSPPGM (Display Program)

These commands manage programs. A program is an executable object
created by a non-ILE high-level language compiler, or by binding
modules together, using CRTPGM. WRKPGM lets you manage
programs using an interactive list. CHGPGM changes certain properties
of a program without recompiling the program. For example, you can use

this command to optimize a program, removing redundant instructions. DLTPGM deletes a program object from the system. DLTPGM deletes any program, regardless of which compiler originally created it (RPG, CL, COBOL, etc.). DSPPGM shows information about a program, including the date and time it was created, and the compiler that created it.

Files Used

CRTPGM:

QSYS/QSYSPRT	*PRTF	Source listing printer file.

DSPPGM:

QSYS/QPDPGM	*PRTF	Program information printer file.

Common MONMSG Messages

CHGPGM:

CPF0540	*USRLIBL not allowed with generic name or *ALL.
CPF0541	Program not changed.
CPF0542	Program not changed.
CPF0543	User not authorized to change program.
CPF0545	No programs changed.
CPF0546	nn changed. nn did not require change. nn not changed.
CPF0547	Cannot remove observable information.
CPF0549	User not authorized to change program.
CPF9806	Cannot perform function for object.
CPF9811	Program not found.
CPF9818	Object not created.
CPF9819	Object not created.
CPF9820	Not authorized to use library.
CPF9821	Not authorized to program.

...

CRTPGM:

CPF3C50	Program not created.
CPF5D12	Error encountered during program or service program preparation.

DLTPGM:

CPF2105	Object not found.
CPF2110	Library not found.
CPF2113	Cannot allocate library.
CPF2114	Cannot allocate object.
CPF2117	nn objects deleted. nn objects not deleted.
CPF2182	Not authorized to library.
CPF2189	Not authorized to object.

...

DSPPGM:

CPF2150	Object information function failed.
CPF2151	Operation failed.
CPF9806	Cannot perform function for object.
CPF9811	Program not found.
CPF9820	Not authorized to use library.
CPF9821	Not authorized to program.

...

WRKPGM:
CPF9809   Library cannot be accessed.
CPF9820   Not authorized to use library.

WRKPNLGRP (Work with Panel Groups)

CRTPNLGRP (Create Panel Group)
DLTPNLGRP (Delete Panel Group)
These commands deal with panel groups. Panel groups are sets of displays defined by User Interface Manager (UIM) source statements instead of Data Description Specifications (DDS). They are commonly used for help displays. WRKPNLGRP lets you work with panel groups using an interactive list display. CRTPNLGRP creates a group of help panels from UIM source in a source physical file member. DLTPNLGRP deletes a panel group.

Files Used

CRTPNLGRP:

QGPL/QPNLSRC	*PF	Source default input file.
QSYS/QSYSPRT	*PRTF	Source listing printer file.

MONMSG Messages

CRTPNLGRP:
CPF5A02   Panel group not created.

DLTPNLGRP:
CPF2114   Cannot allocate object.

WRKPNLGRP:
CPF9809   Library cannot be accessed.

WRKRPYLE (Work with System Reply List Entries)

ADDRPYLE (Add Reply List Entry)
CHGRPYLE (Change Reply List Entry)
RMVRPYLE (Remove Reply List Entry)
These commands manage the system message reply list. The system reply list contains default replies to common messages. WRKRPYLE lets you add, change, remove, and print entries in the system reply list. ADDRPYLE adds a system reply list entry. CHGRPYLE changes an entry. RMVRPYLE removes an entry from the reply list.

Files Used

WRKRPYLE:

QSYS/QPRTRPYL	*PRTF	System reply list printer file.

Common MONMSG Messages

(All)
CPF2435   System reply list not found.
CPF2558   System reply list currently in use.
...

ADDRPYLE:
CPF2436   System Reply List entry not added or changed.
CPF2499   Message identifier not allowed.
CPF2555   Sequence number already defined in system reply list.

CHGRPYLE:
CPF2436   System Reply List entry not added or changed.

CPF2499 Message identifier not allowed.
CPF2556 Sequence number not defined in system reply list.
RMVRPYLE:
CPF2556 Sequence number not defined in system reply list.
WRKRPYLE:
CPF9847 Error occurred while closing file.

WRKSBMJOB (Work with Submitted Jobs) — *See WRKJOB*

WRKSBS (Work with Subsystems) — *See also WRKJOB, WRKSBSD*
ENDSBS (End Subsystem)
STRSBS (Start Subsystem)
These commands manage subsystems on the AS/400. A subsystem is an
environment, described by a subsystem description, in which jobs run.
WRKSBS uses an interactive list display to let you work with active
subsystems. STRSBS starts a subsystem; ENDSBS ends a subsystem.

Common MONMSG Messages
ENDSBS:
CPF1032 System ending with *CNTRLD option.
CPF1033 System ending with *IMMED option.
CPF1034 All subsystems ending with *CNTRLD option.
CPF1035 Subsystems ending with *IMMED option.
CPF1036 System powering down with *CNTRLD option.
CPF1037 System powering down with *IMMED option.
CPF1038 No authority to use command.
CPF1052 ENDSBS *ALL not allowed in current environment.
CPF1053 Ending controlling subsystem &1 not allowed.
CPF1054 No subsystem active.
CPF1055 Subsystem ending with *CNTRLD option.
CPF1056 Subsystem already ending with *IMMED option.
CPF1081 Controlling subsystem already ending to a single job.
...

STRSBS:
CPF1004 Function check occurred during start subsystem.
CPF1010 Subsystem name active.
CPF1011 Start subsystem failed.
CPF1012 No authority to start subsystem.
CPF1013 Subsystem not found.
CPF1014 Subsystem not started.
CPF1031 Not authorized to library.
CPF1049 Cannot allocate subsystem.
CPF1050 Not enough storage to start subsystem.
CPF1067 Cannot allocate library.
CPF1080 Library not found.
CPF1086 Subsystem allocated to your job.
CPF1099 Subsystem not started because system ending.
...

WRKSBS:
CPF9847 Error occurred while closing file.
CPF9850 Override of printer file not allowed.
CPF9851 Overflow value for file too small.

WRKSBSD (Work with Subsystem Descriptions) — *See also*
WRKJOBQ, WRKSBS
ADDJOBQE (Add Job Queue Entry)

CHGJOBQE (Change Job Queue Entry)
CHGSBSD (Change Subsystem Description)
CRTSBSD (Create Subsystem Description)
DLTSBSD (Delete Subsystem Description)
DSPSBSD (Display Subsystem Description)
RMVJOBQE (Remove Job Queue Entry)

These commands deal with subsystem descriptions. A subsystem description names and defines an environment in which jobs run. WRKSBSD works with susbsystem descriptions, using an interactive list display. CRTSBSD creates a subsystem description. CHGSBSD changes some of the attributes of an existing subsystem. DSPSBSD shows the properties and characteristics of an existing subsystem description. DLTSBSD deletes an existing subsystem description from the system.

One of the properties of a subsystem description is the job queue entry. A subsystem may have one or more job queue entries, which name the job queues that provide jobs to a subsystem. ADDJOBQE adds a new job queue entry. CHGJOBQE changes some of the attributes of a job queue entry. RMVJOBQE removes a job queue entry from a subsystem description (but does not remove the subsystem description or the job queue from the system).

Files Used

DSPSBSD:

QSYS/QPRTSBSD	*PRTF	Subsystem description printer file.

Common MONMSG Messages

(All except CRTSBSD, DLTSBSD, DSPSBSD, WRKSBSD)
CPF1697   Subsystem description not changed.
...

CHGSBSD:
CPF1691   Active subsystem description may or may not have changed.

CRTSBSD:
CPF1696   Subsystem description not created.
CPF1699   Subsystem description created, but warnings exist.

DLTSBSD:
CPF2105   Object not found.
CPF2110   Library not found.
CPF2114   Cannot allocate object.
CPF2117   nn objects deleted. nn objects not deleted.
CPF2160   Object type not eligible for requested function.
CPF2182   Not authorized to library.
CPF2189   Not authorized to object.
...

DSPSBSD:
CPF1692   Subsystem description not displayed.
CPF9850   Override of printer file not allowed.
CPF9851   Overflow value for file too small.
CPF9861   Output file created.
...

WRKSBSD:
CPF9809   Library cannot be accessed.

WRKSBSJOB (Work with Subsystem Jobs) — *See WRKJOB*

WRKSPLF (Work with Spooled Files)
CHGSPLFA (Change Spooled File Attributes)
CPYSPLF (Copy Spooled File)
DLTSPLF (Delete Spooled File)
DSPSPLF (Display Spooled File)
HLDSPLF (Hold Spooled File)
RLSSPLF (Release Spooled File)
WRKSPLFA (Work with Spooled File Attributes)

These commands deal with spooled files and their attributes. A spooled file is usually a report waiting on an output queue. WRKSPLF manipulates a user's spooled files, using an interactive list display. CPYSPLF copies the records in a spooled file to a database file. DLTSPLF removes a spooled file from the output queue. DSPSPLF displays the contents of a spooled file, letting you look at a report on the display. HLDSPLF holds a spooled file, so that it cannot print until it is released. RLSSPLF releases a held or saved spool file for printing.

WRKSPLFA displays the current attributes of a spooled file; these attributes include such things as the output queue name, form type, and number of copies to print. CHGSPLFA lets you change some of the spooled file attributes.

Files Used

WRKSPLF:

QSYS/QPRTSPLF	*PRTF	Spooled files printer file.

WRKSPLFA:

QSYS/QPDSPSFA	*PRTF	Spooled file attributes printer file.

Common MONMSG Messages

(All except WRKSPLF)

CPF3303	File not found.
CPF3309	No files with specified name are active.
CPF3330	Necessary resource not available.
CPF3340	More than one file with specified name found.
CPF3342	Job not found.
CPF3343	Duplicate job names found.
CPF3344	File no longer in the system.

CHGSPLFA:

CPF2207	Not authorized to use object.
CPF3335	File attributes not changed.
CPF3341	File attributes not changed.
CPF33C6	Priority required to move file exceeds user's limit.
CPF33C7	Cannot move file ahead of other users' files.
CPF33D0	Printer does not exist.
CPF33D1	User does not exist.
CPF33F0	Not authorized to move spooled file.
CPF3401	Cannot change COPIES for files in PRT status.
CPF3464	Not authorized to output queue.
CPF3492	Not authorized to spooled file.

CPYSPLF:

CPF2207	Not authorized to use object.
CPF3207	Member not added. Errors occurred.
CPF3311	Copy request failed.
CPF3394	Cannot convert spooled file data.
CPF3429	File cannot be displayed, copied, or sent.

CPF3482　Copy request failed. Spool file is open.
CPF3483　Copy request failed.
CPF3492　Not authorized to spooled file.
CPF5812　Member already exists.
CPF9812　File not found.
...

DLTSPLF:
CPF33D0　Printer does not exist.
CPF33D1　User does not exist.
CPF3478　File not found.
CPF3492　Not authorized to spooled file.
CPF34A4　File not held or deleted.

DSPSPLF:
CPF2207　Not authorized to use object.
CPF3308　Error occurred when trying to display data.
CPF3359　Not able to display data.
CPF3386　File not a data base file.
CPF3387　Cannot display data in file.
CPF3394　Cannot convert spooled file data.
CPF3427　Not interactive job.
CPF3428　DSPSPLF command ended for file.
CPF3429　File cannot be displayed, copied, or sent.
CPF3434　Data not in required format.
CPF3435　Requested data not found.
CPF3478　File not found.
CPF3492　Not authorized to spooled file.
CPF9812　File not found.
CPF9815　Member not found.

HLDSPLF:
CPF3337　File already held or saved.
CPF33D0　Printer does not exist.
CPF33D1　User does not exist.
CPF3492　Not authorized to spooled file.
CPF34A4　File not held or deleted.

RLSSPLF:
CPF3304　File cannot be released.
CPF3322　File not released.
CPF33D0　Printer does not exist.
CPF33D1　User does not exist.
CPF3492　Not authorized to spooled file.

WRKSPLF:
CPF1E94　User name does not exist.
CPF1E95　Printer not found.
CPF1E99　Unexpected error occurred.
CPF3302　Override of print file not valid.
CPF3330　Necessary resource not available.
CPF33D0　Printer does not exist.
CPF33D1　User does not exist.
...

WRKSPLFA:
CPF3302　Override of print file not valid.
CPF3336　Job no longer in the system.

WRKSPLFA (Work with Spooled File Attributes) — *See WRKSPLF*

WRKSRVPGM (Work with Service Programs)

CHGSRVPGM (Change Service Program)
CRTSRVPGM (Create Service Program)
DLTSRVPGM (Delete Service Program)
DSPSRVPGM (Display Service Program)

These commands manage service programs. A service program is a bound program that can provide utility subroutine-like functions to other bound programs. WRKSRVPGM lets you manage service programs using an interactive list. CRTSRVPGM creates a service program from a set of modules and binding directories. CHGSRVPGM changes certain properties of a service program, without re-creating the program. DLTSRVPGM deletes a service program from the system, and DSPSRVPGM displays certain information about a service program.

Files Used

CRTSRVPGM, DSPSRVPGM:

QSYS/QSYSPRT   *PRTF   Printer file.

Common MONMSG Messages

CHGSRVPGM:

CPF5CEB   Service program not found.
CPF5CEC   nn changed. nn did not require change. nn not changed.
CPF5CED   No service programs changed.
CPF5CEF   *USRLIBL not allowed with generic name or *ALL.
CPF5CF0   User not authorized.
CPF5CF1   Cannot remove observable information.
CPF5CF2   User not authorized.
CPF5CF3   Service program not changed.
CPF5CF4   Service program not changed.
...

CRTSRVPGM:

CPF5D05   Service program not created.
CPF5D12   Error encountered during program or service program preparation.

DLTSRVPGM:

(None)

DSPSRVPGM:

CPF2150   Object information function failed.
CPF2151   Operation failed.
CPF9801   Object not found.
CPF9802   Not authorized to object.
CPF9806   Cannot perform function for object.
CPF9820   Not authorized to use library.
...

WRKSRVPGM:

(None)

WRKSYSSTS (Work with System Status)

DSPSYSSTS (Display System Status)

These commands display or print information about the current status of the system, including disk usage information, and main storage pool

---

information. In addition to showing information, WRKSYSSTS lets you change main storage allocations.

Files Used

QSYS/QPDSPSTS   *PRTF   System status printer file.

MONMSG Messages

DSPSYSSTS:

(None)

WRKSYSSTS:

CPF1009	Statistics elapsed time too long. Start time reset.
CPF1882	Value for paging option not valid.
CPF9847	Error occurred while closing file.
CPF9850	Override of printer file not allowed.
CPF9851	Overflow value for file too small.

WRKSYSVAL (Work with System Values)

CHGSYSVAL (Change System Value)
DSPSYSVAL (Display System Value)
RTVSYSVAL (Retrieve System Value)

These commands deal with system values. System values are characteristics common to the entire system that let you control and customize certain operating system functions, such as the date and time. WRKSYSVAL offers an interactive list display to let you change or display system values. DSPSYSVAL shows the current value of a system value; CHGSYSVAL lets you change the value of a system value. RTVSYSVAL retrieves the current value of a system value, placing it into a CL program variable, identified by the RTNVAR parameter.

Files Used

DSPSYSVAL:

QSYS/QPDSPSVL   *PRTF   System values printer file.

WRKSYSVAL:

QSYS/QSYSPRT   *PRTF   System values printer file.

Common MONMSG Messages

(All except WRKSYSVAL)

CPF1028   Invalid SYSVAL parameter.

...

CHGSYSVAL:

CPF1030	System value cannot be changed.
CPF1058	VALUE parameter not correct.
CPF1059	Length of value not correct.
CPF1076	Specified value not allowed.
CPF1078	System value not changed.
CPF1079	Too many or too few values listed.
CPF1127	Device specified for QPRTDEV not printer device.
CPF1132	Name specified not valid.
CPF1203	Keyboard identifier not correct.
CPF1830	Specified values not valid.
CPF1831	User not authorized to change system value.
CPF1832	Cannot change system value during IPL.
CPF1842	Cannot access system value.
CPF1852	System value not changed.
CPF1856	Filter type not correct.
CPF1857	Specified value not a code font.

CPF1864   User not authorized to change system value.
CPF268D   Unable to access system value.
...

DSPSYSVAL:
CPF9847   Error occurred while closing file.
CPF9850   Override of printer file not allowed.
CPF9851   Overflow value for file too small.

RTVSYSVAL:
CPF1094   CL variable not same type as system value.
CPF1095   CL variable length not valid for system value.
CPF1842   Cannot access system value.
CPF268D   Unable to access system value.

WRKSYSVAL:
CPF1030   System value cannot be changed.
CPF1059   Length of value not correct.
CPF1076   Specified value not allowed.
CPF1078   System value not changed.
CPF1079   Too many or too few values listed.
CPF1203   Keyboard identifier not correct.
CPF1831   User not authorized to change system value.
CPF1852   System value not changed.
CPF1856   Filter type not correct.
CPF1857   Specified value not a code font.
CPF1864   User not authorized to change system value.
...

WRKUSRJOB (Work with User Jobs) — *See WRKJOB*

WRKUSRPRF (Work with User Profiles) — *See also CHGPWD,*
SAVSECDTA
CHGPRF (Change Profile)
CHGUSRPRF (Change User Profile)
CRTUSRPRF (Create User Profile)
DLTUSRPRF (Delete User Profile)
DSPUSRPRF (Display User Profile)
RTVUSRPRF (Retrieve User Profi*le)*

These commands relate to user profiles. A user profile (user ID) is an object that contains information about a user, including the user's password; the system uses the user profile to verify a user's authorities and to customize certain functions. WRKUSRPRF manipulates one or more user profiles, using a convenient list display. CRTUSRPRF creates a new user profile. CHGPRF changes some of the information in your own profile. CHGUSRPRF changes some of the information in any user profile. DLTUSRPRF removes a user profile from the system. DSPUSRPRF shows certain information about a user.

RTVUSRPRF retrieves information about a user, placing the information into one or more CL program variables. Use the following parameters to retrieve the information:

ACGCDE	*CHAR 15	Accounting code.
ASTLVL	*CHAR 10	Assistance level: *SYSVAL, *BASIC, *INTERMED, *ADVANCED.

ATNPGM	*CHAR 10	Default attention key handling program: name, *SYSVAL, *NONE.
ATNPGMLIB	*CHAR 10	ATNPGM library.
AUDLVL	*CHAR 640	Object auditing level entries (up to 64).
CCSID	*DEC (5 0)	Coded character set identifier: identifier, -2 = *SYSVAL.
CNTRYID	*CHAR 10	Country identifier: identifier, *SYSVAL.
CURLIB	*CHAR 10	Current library: name, *CRTDFT.
DLVRY	*CHAR 10	Message control delivery value: *NOTIFY, *BREAK, *HOLD, *DFT.
DSPSGNINF	*CHAR 7	Display sign-on information display: *SYSVAL, *YES, *NO.
GRPPRF	*CHAR 10	Group profile, or *NONE.
GRPAUT	*CHAR 10	Authority granted to group profile for created objects: *NONE, *CHANGE, *ALL, *USE, *EXCLUDE.
INLMNU	*CHAR 10	Initial menu.
INLMNULIB	*CHAR 10	INLMNU library.
INLPGM	*CHAR 10	Initial program.
INLPGMLIB	*CHAR 10	INLPGM library.
JOBD	*CHAR 10	User's job description.
JOBDLIB	*CHAR 10	JOBD library.
KBDBUF	*CHAR 10	Keyboard buffering: *SYSVAL, *NO, *TYPEAHEAD, *YES.
LMTCPB	*CHAR 10	Limit command capability: *NO, *YES, *PARTIAL.
LMTDEVSSN	*CHAR 7	Limit device sessions: *SYSVAL, *YES, *NO.
LANGID	*CHAR 10	Language identifier: identifier, *SYSVAL.
MAXSTG	*DEC (11 0)	Maximum auxiliary storage space allowed. -1 = *NOMAX.
MSGQ	*CHAR 10	Message queue.
MSGQLIB	*CHAR 10	MSGQ library.
NOTVLDSIGN	*DEC (11 0)	Number of invalid sign-on attempts.
OBJAUD	*CHAR 10	Object auditing value: *NONE, *CHANGE, *ALL.
OUTQ	*CHAR 10	Output queue: name, *DEV, *WRKSTN.
OUTQLIB	*CHAR 10	OUTQ library.
OWNER	*CHAR 10	Owner of created objects: *USRPRF or *GRPPRF.

PRTDEV	*CHAR 10		Default printer device: name, *SYSVAL, *WORKSTN.
PRVSIGN	*CHAR 13		Previous sign-on date: CYYMMDDHHMMSS.
PTYLMT	*CHAR 1		Highest JOBPTY and OUTPTY allowed: 0-9.
PWDCHGDAT	*CHAR 6		Last password change date: YYMMDD.
PWDEXP	*CHAR 4		Password expired: *YES, *NO.
PWDEXPITV	*DEC (5 0)		Password expiration interval (days): 1-366, 0 = *SYSVAL, -1 = *NOMAX.
RTNUSRPRF	*CHAR 10		The name of the user profile retrieved.
SEV	*DEC (2 0)		Message control severity level: 00-99.
SPCAUT	*CHAR 100		List of special user authorities, up to 10, each 10 characters long.
SPCENV	*CHAR 10		Special environment: *SYSVAL, *NONE, *S36.
SRTSEQ	*CHAR 10		Sort sequence table identifier: identifier, *HEX, *LANGIDUNQ, *LANGIDSHR, *SYSVAL.
SRTSEQLIB	*CHAR 10		Sort sequence table library.
STATUS	*CHAR 10		User status: *ENABLED, *DISABLED.
STGUSED	*DEC (15 0)		Auxiliary storage space currently used by user, in KB.
TEXT	*CHAR 50		Text description of user profile.
USRCLS	*CHAR 10		User class: *USER, *SYSOPR, *PGMR, *SECADM, *SECOFR.
USROPT	*CHAR 240		User option values (up to 24).

Files Used

DSPUSRPRF:

QSYS/QADSPUPA	*PF	Model OUTFILE for TYPE(*OBJAUT).
QSYS/QADSPUPB	*PF	Model OUTFILE for TYPE(*BASIC).
QSYS/QADSPUPO	*PF	Model OUTFILE for TYPE(*OBJOWN).
QSYS/QPUSRPRF	*PRTF	User profile printer file.

Common MONMSG Messages

(All except WRKUSRPRF)
CPF2213   Not able to allocate user profile.

CHGPRF:

CPF2209	Library not found.
CPF2225	Not able to allocate internal system object.
CPF2228	Not authorized to change user profile.
CPF2242	Object not found in library list.
CPF2244	Object cannot be found.
CPF2294	Initial program value cannot be changed.
CPF2295	Initial menu value cannot be changed.
CPF2296	Attention program value cannot be changed.
CPF2297	Current library value cannot be changed.
CPF9802	Not authorized to object.
CPF9820	Not authorized to use library.
CPF9825	Not authorized to device.

...

CHGUSRPRF:

CPF2201	User password already exists.
CPF2203	User profile not correct.
CPF2204	User profile not found.
CPF2209	Library not found.
CPF2225	Not able to allocate internal system object.
CPF2228	Not authorized to change user profile.
CPF2242	Object not found in library list.
CPF2244	Object cannot be found.
CPF2259	Group profile not found.
CPF2260	User profile cannot be a group profile.
CPF2261	OWNER or GRPAUT value not permitted.
CPF2262	Value for GRPAUT not correct.
CPF2264	User profile not allowed to be a group member.
CPF2269	Special authority *ALLOBJ required when granting *SECADM or *AUDIT.
CPF2272	Cannot allocate user profile.
CPF2292	*SECADM required to create or change user profiles.
CPF22F3	Specified LMTCPB value not permitted.
CPF9802	Not authorized to object.

...

CRTUSRPRF:

CPF2201	User password already exists.
CPF2202	Do not have authority to create user profile.
CPF2209	Library not found.
CPF2212	Not able to allocate library.
CPF2214	User profile already exists.
CPF2225	Not able to allocate internal system object.
CPF2242	Object not found in library list.
CPF2244	Object cannot be found.
CPF2259	Group profile not found.
CPF2260	User profile cannot be a group profile.
CPF2261	OWNER or GRPAUT value not permitted.
CPF2262	Value for GRPAUT not correct.
CPF2269	Special authority *ALLOBJ required when granting *SECADM or *AUDIT.
CPF2292	*SECADM required to create or change user profiles.

CPF22E8	Some objects not deleted. Try again.
CPF22F3	Specified LMTCPB value not permitted.
CPF9802	Not authorized to object.

...

DLTUSRPRF:

CPF2204	User profile not found.
CPF2215	User profile not deleted.
CPF2217	Not authorized to user profile.
CPF2222	Storage limit is greater than specified for user profile.
CPF2225	Not able to allocate internal system object.
CPF2227	One or more errors occurred during processing of command.
CPF2229	Not authorized to delete user profile.
CPF2258	Group profile not deleted.
CPF2263	Group information removed from nn user profiles.
CPF2265	User profile not deleted.
CPF22B3	User profile not deleted.
CPF22BF	User profile not deleted.
CPF22C1	NEWOWN and USRPRF parameters cannot be the same.
CPI2236	Deleting owned objects.

DSPUSRPRF:

CPF2204	User profile not found.
CPF2217	Not authorized to user profile.
CPF2257	User profile not a group profile.
CPF22D8	Use of generic user profile name not correct.
CPF22D9	No user profiles of specified name exist.
CPF9860	Error occurred during output file processing.

RTVUSRPRF:

CPF2203	User profile not correct.
CPF2204	User profile not found.
CPF2217	Not authorized to user profile.
CPF2225	Not able to allocate internal system object.

...

WRKUSRPRF:

CPF1E60	Not authorized to do request.

...

WRKWTR (Work with Writers)

CHGWTR (Change Writer)
ENDWTR (End Writer)
HLDWTR (Hold Writer)
RLSWTR (Release Writer)
STRPRTWTR (Start Printer Writer)

These commands deal with the status of printers and writers. A print writer is the program that enables a printer to print spooled files. STRPRTWTR starts a writer for a printer you specify. CHGWTR changes the form type, number of file separator pages, and/or the output queue for a print writer. HLDWTR temporarily stops a writer, while RLSWTR releases a held writer. ENDWTR permanently stops a writer. WRKWTR manipulates the status of printers and writers, using a convenient list panel display.

Files Used

STRPRTWTR:

QSYS/QSPLPRT	*PRTF	Printer device file.

WRKWTR:

QSYS/QPRTRDWT	*PRTF	Writer printer file.

Common MONMSG Messages

(All)

CPF3330	Necessary resource not available.

CHGWTR:

CPF2207	Not authorized to use object.
CPF3313	Writer not active nor on job queue.
CPF3331	Not authorized to control writer.
CPF3357	Output queue not found.
CPF3456	Cannot change writer to output queue.
CPF3457	Cannot change writer.
CPF3458	Change writer not allowed. End writer pending.
CPF3459	Writer not eligible for change.
CPF3460	Change writer not allowed.
CPF3463	Output queue not found.
CPF3464	Not authorized to output queue.

...

ENDWTR:

CPF1317	No response from subsystem for job.
CPF1340	Job control function not performed.
CPF1352	Function not done. Job in transition condition.
CPF1842	Cannot access system value.
CPF3313	Writer not active nor on job queue.
CPF3331	Not authorized to control writer.
CPF3339	Previous end request to writer pending.

...

HLDWTR:

CPF1340	Job control function not performed.
CPF3313	Writer not active nor on job queue.
CPF3331	Not authorized to control writer.
CPF3332	Writer already held.
CPF3334	Previous hold to writer pending.

....

RLSWTR:

CPF1317	No response from subsystem for job.
CPF1340	Job control function not performed.
CPF1352	Function not done. Job in transition condition.
CPF3313	Writer not active nor on job queue.
CPF3316	Writer not released because writer not held.
CPF3331	Not authorized to control writer.
CPF3334	Previous hold to writer pending.

...

STRPRTWTR:

CPF1338	Errors occurred on SBMJOB command.
CPF1764	Writer already started for device.
CPF1842	Cannot access system value.
CPF2207	Not authorized to use object.
CPF3303	File not found in job.

CPF3305	Output queue assigned to another writer.
CPF3309	No files named are active.
CPF3310	Writer already started.
CPF3340	More than one file with specified name found in job.
CPF3342	Job not found.
CPF3343	Duplicate job names found.
CPF3347	Device not found.
CPF3357	Output queue not found.
CPF3363	Message queue not found.
CPF3369	Device not printer device.
CPF3463	Output queue for device not found.
CPF3464	Not authorized to output queue.
CPF3478	File not found.

...

WRKWTR:

CPF0941	Job no longer in system.
CPF1070	Job not found.
CPF1071	No authority to job.
CPF1E99	Unexpected error occurred.
CPF3302	Override of print file not valid.
CPF3313	Writer not active nor on job queue.
CPF3330	Necessary resource not available.
CPF3336	Job no longer in the system.

...